Success for Modern Day Relationships

Success for Modern Day Relationships

*Working with Dating, Engaged,
and Married Couples*

Barbara R. Cohl, PhD

JASON ARONSON
Lanham • Boulder • New York • Toronto • Plymouth, UK

Published by Jason Aronson
A wholly owned subsidiary of The Rowman & Littlefield Publishing Group, Inc.
4501 Forbes Boulevard, Suite 200, Lanham, Maryland 20706
www.rowman.com

10 Thornbury Road, Plymouth PL6 7PP, United Kingdom

British Library Cataloguing in Publication Information Available

Library of Congress Cataloging-in-Publication Data

Cohl, Barbara R., 1949-
Success for modern day relationships : working with dating, engaged, and married couples / Barbara
R. Cohl.
p. cm.
Includes bibliographical references and index.
ISBN 978-0-7657-0925-7 (cloth : alk. paper) -- ISBN 978-0-7657-0926-4 (electronic)
1. Marriage counseling. 2. Couples--Counseling of. I. Title.
HQ10.C577 2012
616.89'1562--dc23
2011053369

Printed in the United States of America

I want to dedicate this book to my husband, Dr. Robert Katz for being so encouraging and supportive throughout the writing and publishing of my book. I also want to express much appreciation to my patients who have taught me so much about relationships. The sharing of their experiences and the trust they had of my dedication to them cannot be measured in words.

Contents

Acknowledgments

I have sincere gratitude to the following people who helped make writing and publishing this book both a labor of love and a joy:

My husband Robert Katz, PhD, who is an excellent psychologist and who provided me with his insights and experiences that served to enrich my own.

My editor, Amy King, for being interested in my ideas and who made the editing of my book so amazingly easy and pleasant.

My publisher, Jason Aronson, for accepting and publishing my book.

Introduction

We enjoy our work as relationship and marital therapists. We have the opportunity to meet wonderful people who are devoted to changing their lives for the better. We feel complimented that they have chosen us to help them with this incredible task. They demonstrate much faith and trust in telling us their most precious secrets. They share intimate details about their relationships. Most of these details have not been shared with others, not even with their spouses. We take their trust and their willingness to discuss their life experiences with us very seriously. We devote much time and energy to provide the utmost in ethical and professional services. This is our pledge to our patients.

In conversations with our patients, we have referred to the therapy we offer as *spa for the mind.* To some, this may sound quirky or new age, but let me explain. Many people go to the spa for a massage, a facial, a manicure, or other services. They leave this setting feeling refreshed and relaxed. There is no question that these services are helpful, and we recommend them to our patients because we believe that they ought to take the time to pamper themselves.

Our *spa* services are special as well. Our patients have the opportunity to speak their minds and their hearts in a setting in which we listen attentively to every word they say. We are totally focused on them for fifty minutes. There are no distractions or demands on their time. They are not criticized or judged. They receive feedback in a constructive and supportive manner. They are given understanding, caring, and empathy. They have the opportunity to receive the advice of professionals who do not have any hidden agenda or competing interests.

To enhance their *spa* experience, we create a very inviting and quiet setting. We offer comfortable seating, soft lights, scented candles, table fountains, and our candy dish is always full. So when I ask our patients where else they can get such a pleasant experience, they are quick to acknowledge that our services are indeed *spa for the mind*.

Another service that we provide our patients is the usefulness of our experience as husband and wife. We find it helpful to *model* our own relationship as a healthy, happy couple who is able to acknowledge our own conflicts and address them successfully. We are clearly able to tell our patients what we would do if we had a similar situation. It seems that our patients trust our opinions. They are also comforted by the fact that they have a healthy couple to guide them as they face a difficult road in marital therapy.

Indeed sometimes we function as their *pain sponges*. We are there to listen to their stories and to see them through their toughest battles. We allow ourselves to essentially absorb their pain and frustrations. We then take these embattled feelings and come up with ideas and make suggestions that are constructive and meaningful to their relationships. We help them rise from their despair and hopelessness. We give them solid advice and teach them techniques that have helped other couples strengthen their ties and conquer their weaknesses. Indeed, we teach them to use the tools and techniques that happy couples have mastered.

In this book, we refer to both relationship and marital therapy. The two terms are not synonymous. Relationship therapy is provided to those who are not married. They may be dating or engaged to be married. We have found that the techniques we teach our patients are applicable to other relationships as well. Our patients have told us that they are able to successfully use these methods in their relationships with co-workers, supervisors, family members, friends, and neighbors. So when we refer to *relationship therapy*, we are describing techniques that are helpful for everyone who interacts with others. I dare say that includes most if not all of us.

When we use the term marital therapy we are referring to couples that are legally and/or spiritually married. With these couples we adapt our techniques so they are appropriate to those persons who share a deep intimate connection and commitment to one another.

We teach useful methods to resolve conflicts, clearly and fairly express their needs, establish healthy boundaries, provide constructive and fair feedback, receive feedback with grace and dignity, establish reachable goals, and create realistic expectations for themselves and others. We provide fun and effective lessons on flirting with a special love interest. We instruct our patients on how to be a great date so they are asked out again and again. We count on our happy couples to describe how to have a successful relationship that can pass the test of time.

All of the couples that enter relationship or marital therapy are in search of a definite change and an improvement in their relationships. They may be at a crossroads and need help to determine whether to stay together or go their separate ways. Some couples enter therapy because they simply cannot go another day, week, or month without expressing how unhappy they are with their partners or perhaps with their lives in general. They want help, and they want it now. Of course we inform them that change does not occur overnight. Relationship and marital therapy is a process, a journey, often painful, and often successful. We add that successful therapy does not depend on whether the couple stays together. We are pleased when our couples are able to resolve their difficulties and choose to stay together. Yet we have found that successful therapy could also mean that the couple has discovered that they are happier being single than together. A couple is successful when they have realized that they each have the skills and the strengths to create a new path on their own. Sometimes a couple realizes that they have changed so much that they no longer feel compatible with their mate. Perhaps they no longer have the same needs, goals, or dreams. Perhaps they no longer love each other enough to stay together. When this type of understanding or decision is reached, a couple may separate or divorce. In therapy, they hopefully will develop an improved understanding of what caused the relationship to end.

In chapter 1 we refer to the phrase created by Dr. Katz, *you cannot fight until you are ready to lose.* This refers to our couples that realize that they must be one hundred percent committed to fighting for their relationship. They must be honest, open, loyal, and willing to devote much time and energy to use the techniques we teach them in their therapy sessions. These same couples also realize that despite *the good fight*, their relationship may not survive. Knowing this fact gives our couples the freedom to fight *the good fight*. They are aware of the possibility that they may or may not stay together. During the course of therapy, they learn that they will survive, they will endure, and they will move on with their lives regardless of the fate of their relationships.

In the upcoming chapters in this book, you will meet many couples that have had challenges in their relationships. The names and circumstances of these individuals have been altered to protect their anonymity. Some of the dialogs have been specially created to make a specific point or teach skills that our happy couples have mastered in both therapy and in life.

For those who are considering picking up the phone and calling a therapist, we offer you our support. It is a difficult decision to make. Once you begin this experience, it is more harmful to pull away and quit therapy prematurely. You see, once important issues have been presented, it is not

healthy to allow them to essentially *hang in the air* without making a sufficient effort to resolve them. It would be similar to a surgeon opening a
wound and neglecting to suture it shut.

Relationship and marital therapy is a wonderful opportunity to strengthen
a strong relationship or marriage. Many of our couples have solid relationships or marriages, but believe that therapy can make them even better. They
want to learn new skills to enhance their marriages. Other couples seek
therapy to address a significant stressor in their lives. They want to insure
that life events do not cause problems in their relationships. These couples
may come and go in and out of therapy as a response to the ups and downs
that are present in all relationships.

Of course there are couples that enter relationship or marital therapy to
address infidelity, control issues, addictions, abuse, major conflicts, or that
they have grown apart, and no longer share the same interests and values they
had in the beginning of their relationship.

We are open to treat all couples that are amenable to therapy and are
willing to take the time and make the effort to devote to treatment. To all of
our couples, past, present, and future, we wish you peace, happiness, and a
positive experience in relationship or marital therapy. We hope you can join
the ranks of the happy couples that have contributed to this book.

*The readers will notice that I use the word *we* quite often when I describe the marital and relationship therapy that I offer. I have written this
book with the consultation of my psychologist husband Dr. Robert Katz. At
times we see patients together, at other times we see them separately. We are
always a telephone call away when faced with a difficult case. To honor our
collaboration, I use the word *we*, as *we* are a couple for life.

Chapter One

Time for a Change

When couples enter into marriage, they are hopeful their unions will last. Most couples believe they will not fall prey to the climbing statistics that indicate approximately 40 percent of marriages will fail. They believe they will beat the odds and remain in wedded bliss to the end of their days. For too many couples, it is most unsettling to find out the dream of wedded bliss is just that, a dream.

Many husbands and wives drift apart for various reasons. One reason has to do with the reason they got married. If an individual has an unrealistic idea of marriage or commitment, they may be quite disappointed when they have their first quarrel, have to tolerate their mate's poor personal habits, find out their mate has financial problems, or must spend time with their annoying in-laws.

MYTHS THAT PROMPT PEOPLE TO MARRY

Loneliness

Some individuals marry because they fear loneliness. They imagine a life without a partner as intolerable. We meet many single individuals who reach their thirties or forties, and fear that "this is it," they will be single for life. They believe they will not have the opportunity to have children. They experience genuine panic at the idea that, for some reason, they were not good enough, attractive enough, smart enough, or successful enough, to attract a mate. Many believe they are "damaged goods," and must face life alone. These beliefs cause many single individuals to lower the standards they once had for a mate, and accept someone who they do not genuinely love, or someone who does not meet their needs or share their life goals. They may ignore the *red flags* that are present in their relationships. The *red flags* are the warning signs of problems in a relationship that should be addressed as soon as they appear. Instead, many people push aside these warnings, excuse them, or simply don't see them. Instead, they tolerate behavior that is best not tolerated just so they have someone with whom to spend their lives.

Rebounders

We have met many patients who eventually marry because they cannot tolerate being alone. Being alone is quite frightening. To ease their relationship anxiety, they are often in and out of relationships that are largely self-serving due, in part, to their unhealthy dependency needs, or perhaps a chronic need for attention. They always seem to find an individual to date quite soon after a break-up. Although we recommend they do not rebound, they cannot remain "single" for more than a matter of a few weeks. For some of these individuals, being alone on a Saturday night or on a holiday represents being a "failure." These singles may marry to ease their loneliness or fear of being alone. Their hope is to always have a loving partner by their side, but their dependency needs and clingy behaviors may cause potential partners to pull away from them.

Tradition

Many individuals we have met marry out of tradition. They state that everyone in their family, as well as close friends and co-workers, is paired up. After a person attends one too many weddings, parties, and family functions alone, he or she may want to marry to essentially "fit in" with the others in their social circle. They may get much pressure from their family members to marry. They sense there is a hidden message that there is something "wrong" with unmarried individuals. They may be pressured from parents and grandparents to have children, to bring a mate or partner to Thanksgiving dinner. There is pressure from co-workers to attend after hours social events with someone special because many of the co-workers are composed of couples. For many, getting married can provide a feeling of reassurance and "fitting in" to one's social group.

Feeling Complete

Another reason a person may marry is to feel complete. There remains a belief among individuals that a life partner can make someone whole. That one must have a life partner to compliment them; every "ying" must have a "yang." Their notion is that a single person is only half without someone with whom to live with each day. This is often a belief that is passed on by family members and close friends who share this philosophy of life.

No One Else Will Want Me

A person who has had a series of rejections or "bad luck in love," may cling to someone who finds them lovable. This person is often accepting of the notion that they will never find love again. Perhaps they are less attractive than their peers, less occupationally successful, or come from a home in which they have been emotionally neglected or abused. Some of the patients in our practice have been brought up by a single parent. If perhaps the patient is a female whose father left the family, the patient may believe he left because she was not good enough or worth it for him to stay with his family. The false belief often stated is that if her own father did not want her, then it is unlikely anyone else will find her worthy to love. She will believe she is "damaged goods" and "unlovable." So when love does come along, some-times with warts and all, the patient will cling to this person as her perceived one and only chance at love.

Marry the Parent of Your Child

There are those who believe that if you are pregnant or have had a child with a particular person, you should marry that person. One idea that is shared in therapy is to avoid bringing shame to oneself and to their family. Another belief is that each child should live with both of his or her parents in order to grow up to be emotionally healthy. The reality is that this type of union does not necessarily result in a compatible, healthy, happy, and sound relationship. To bring up a child in an unhappy environment, devoid of love, respect, or happiness can be more detrimental to a child than bringing the child up with one parent. We know of many individuals who are quite capable of parenting a child on their own or with the assistance of family and friends. We are not stating that one should not marry the parent of their unborn child. Rather we are suggesting it is important that the relationship is healthy before walking down the aisle.

Due to a Lengthy Relationship

There are couples who marry because they have been dating for a long period of time and think marriage must be the next step. This often occurs between individuals who have dated throughout high school and/or college. The indi-viduals have become comfortable with each other. They may also believe family and friends *expect* them to marry. They have trouble believing they have wasted several years dating an individual if the relationship does not result in marriage. Another reason these individuals marry is because they fear the vastness of the dating scene they may not have witnessed for some time. They fear dating individuals they may have just met. To them, familiar is better, familiar is easier.

To Escape from Unpleasantness

There are individuals who marry to escape an unpleasant living situation. A young person who has recently graduated from high school may marry to leave an unhappy life with her parents. She may believe marriage will allow her the freedom and security she craves. Others marry to seek love and romance, but have an unrealistic idea that "love conquers all," that love can solve all problems, and of course that love "makes the world go round." They believe marriage will complete the picture of what they perceive is missing in their lives. Many individuals believe love equals compatibility. They don't realize a person can truly love her mate, but not be able to tolerate living with him due to differences in lifestyle and goals, among other things.

GROWING PAINS

It is clear to all of us, that when we marry to ease loneliness, to fit into a social group, to meet the expectations of others, or to fill an emotional or social void in our lives, we will possibly make a mistake that may result in unhappiness and ultimately separation or divorce. So what happens when we evolve in our lives and realize the reasons for which we married a particular individual are no longer valid? What happens when we are no longer motivated by loneliness, the dictates of others, or a perceived need for a mate to complete us? An individual's growth and change happens slowly and gradually. Often there are obvious changes in behavior that signal these changes are occurring. By exploring new interests, making new friends, and reaching desired goals, some individuals may find they have moved beyond or away from their mate and the special relationship that suited them in prior years. Now they find the special relationship has grown old and uninteresting. In addition, stressors such as raising a family, financial concerns, job pressures, health issues, and retirement, to name a few, can strain a once strong relationship to a breaking point. Our patients observe that they become concerned when their mate or partner becomes more distant or perhaps more easily agitated. There is less affection, conversation, or emotional sharing and closeness. Other signs and signals of a relationship in trouble are even more devastating such as the realization of an affair, or that life savings, once designated for retirement, are depleted without a trace or explanation.

A Relationship at a Crossroads

So what happens when a couple find themselves at a crossroads? What is a couple to do when they are faced with the choice of staying together in an increasingly stressful and unhappy relationship, or moving on to paths unknown? For many, the familiar remains the lesser of the two evils.

We met with Brad and Emily who had been married for thirty years. Brad had many extramarital affairs. To date, Emily was not aware of Brad's infidelity, but she was aware of their mutual unhappiness in their relationship. In fact, everyone who came in contact with them was aware of their marital woes. Brad continually rolled his eyes when Emily told a joke or recounted a story. He seemed easily bored and annoyed with her. In turn, Emily criticized Brad for everything. Emily would say "no" to Brad's attempts to solidify their relationship by being playful, his desire to go out and have fun together, or take a much-needed vacation. The couple discussed divorce many times, but decided to wait until their children were grown before making this decision. Even though their children, ages twenty and twenty-five, were continuing their education, Brad and Emily decided to postpone getting their divorce until after their children were settled in their careers. They did not continue in marital therapy beyond a few weeks, because they both felt there was not much to work on since their impending divorce was one thing they agreed would take place sometime in the future.

My husband told me a joke about a senior couple, ages ninety-nine and one hundred. They got married when the woman turned sixteen. Their first year of marriage was happy. Since then they have been miserable with each other. When asked why they have stayed together for so long, the husband announced, "We were waiting for our children to die."

We may chuckle at the senior couple's twisted idea of "till death do us part," but Brad and Emily exemplify real life couples that have accomplished their career goals, raised their families, and collected the possessions that define a comfortable life. They know their spouse's faults and positive traits. This familiarity may breed contempt, but it may also stand for the stability and the comfort that exemplifies a predictable life. To leave a predictable or seemingly comfortable life may create a tremendous risk, emotional turmoil, and an inconceivable amount of adjustment and pain. To avoid this discomfort, unhappy couples like Brad and Emily choose to stay together indefinitely.

Facing Change in a Relationship

Many couples consider the idea of change as foreboding, regardless of their accomplishments in life. Although Marcie and Bill were only married for eight years, they quickly adopted a routine that defined their marital relationship. Saturday afternoons were devoted to food shopping and chores. Every Sunday was spent with Marcie's family. Weekday evenings were devoted to scrapbook projects, PTA meetings, and volunteering at a local mission. Bill was bored with their routine, but obediently went along with the status quo.

One day at work, he was talking to a co-worker about a motorcycle club that was planning a trip to New England. Bill listened as his co-worker described the fun trips he had taken with the club over the years. Bill decided to suggest he and Marcie consider joining the club over dinner that evening. Bill explained the club members were upstanding members of the community who were not "bikers" per se. He thought it would be a fun way to make new friends, explore the countryside, and enjoy exciting adventures. Marcie did not agree with his point of view. She reacted strongly to the idea of becoming a "biker chick." She argued that she enjoyed spending their weekends doing chores and visiting with her family. She resisted any change to their routine, and was disappointed that Bill found fault with the way they had always spent their weekends. Bill felt angry with her resistance to change and grow. He also felt trapped by his own need to avoid conflict with her. His tendency was to "go with the flow" in order to avoid confrontation, disagreements, and consequent tension in their relationship.

We suggested they resolve this difficult struggle in one of three ways: (1) Bill would not suggest change in their relationship, and would somehow accept the status quo for the foreseeable future. (2) Marcie would sacrifice her need for sameness and control and follow Bill's lead toward a change in their routine. (3) Marcie and Bill would go their separate ways.

For Marcie and Bill, the result was a continuation of life as they lived it for the past eight years. Neither Marcie, nor Bill was ready to take a risk and fight for a change that had the potential to make their relationship stronger and more enjoyable, or end a relationship that allowed them a sense of security and togetherness. Their need for the status quo was only a temporary postponement of the inevitable expression of tension and resentment that would follow in the years to come.

We all know individuals who prefer to live their lives in the same way year after year. They find solace in having an existence that is seamless from one day to the next. Despite their unhappiness, they tend to keep the same friends, participate in the same activities, and remain in the same unsatisfying job from one year to the next, decade after decade. They may even choose to dress in the same clothes and wear the same hairstyle to avoid the threat of change, the challenge of movement, an ultimate need for control, and the consequences, although positive, of personal development. For these individuals, the concept of change is unimaginable. They have shaped a relationship in which deep patterns of behavior are permanently established. They have worked hard and spent much time to create their own special stamp on their relationship. It is their brand of interacting, reacting, and enduring a status quo even though the relationship is no longer working.

Indeed, change tends to disturb our sense of balance. Change results in our feeling out of control. We may fear if we change any aspect of our lives, our behavior, our appearance, or even our expectations of our spouse, that life as we know it may become unrecognizable. Many of us respond with anxiety and stress when familiar patterns in our lives change. In addition, many of us fear rejection from our spouse if we attempt to introduce or request change in a relationship. Once a spouse voices discontent and a desire to change, the other spouse may feel threatened by the expectation that they must respond one way or another. If they favorably respond to the request, then both parties can begin their new challenging journey together. If one spouse votes against his or her partner's request for change, then the relationship is in conflict unless there is compromise, or the spouse who has requested the change withdraws the request.

Discomfort in a Relationship

For increasing numbers of individuals, the comfort of the status quo proves to be too uncomfortable. Discomfort in a relationship tends to create its own brand of unhappiness and tension. One partner generally feels the discomfort more than the other. The partner who has expressed a desire for a profound change in the relationship may suggest they see a marital therapist. When the couple comes in for their first session we tell them they both must agree to work on the problem for marital therapy to work. In addition, we tell the couple they must be aware that the possible outcome of marital therapy is divorce. During the course of therapy, the couple may learn they are not compatible, and are less happy together than they would be if they were single. This awareness is terribly frightening, as the married couple may choose to avoid conflict. They may hesitate to state what they dislike about their partner. They may be fearful to announce what changes they would like to see in their relationship. They may believe it is unfair or feel embarrassed to bring up a complaint they have harbored for many years, perhaps since they were dating.

Fear of Change

Dana and Martin were married for fourteen years. In an individual therapy session, Dana disclosed to me that she disliked the fact that Martin smoked cigarettes. She conceded that Martin was a polite smoker and only smoked outdoors. Yet she disliked how his clothing and breath smelled after he finished smoking. She disliked how the smell of smoke permeated the house and his car after he smoked a cigarette.

I suggested that Dana tell Martin how she felt, and request that he quit smoking. I further suggested she support him by praising any effort he made to abide by her request. Dana remarked that she couldn't ask him to quit now. She stated that it was "too late." She explained she regretted that she didn't take a stronger stand against his habit when they were dating or first married.

Dana decided to silently endure Martin's smoking habit. She continued to resent him for the unpleasant smell of smoke in their home and resented herself more for her failure to speak up years ago when they first became a couple.

I told Dana she was unfair to Martin if she kept her feelings to herself. By doing so, she was not giving him a chance to please her and to quit smoking. I suggested she approach the subject by requesting that he "air out" before coming indoors after smoking, and that he not smoke in the car they both use. Dana's response was to change the subject and discuss other issues that were less stressful to her.

Dana was correct in her assessment that it is always better to set healthy boundaries early in a relationship. It is helpful to tell a potential partner that some of his or her habits are annoying or distracting. Indeed, it is informative to see a partner's reaction and willingness to change or at least compromise when a fair request is made, preferably prior to the marriage ceremony.

Yet Dana was incorrect in assuming that it is ever too late to request a change in a mate's habits. A spouse that seethes in silence may be perpetually unhappy and resentful of her mate. This unhappiness will slowly and definitely create tension and discord in a relationship that may manifest in a variety of destructive ways. A spouse may demonstrate resentment by distancing herself from her mate, or by behaving in a passive aggressive manner. This may include forgetting a birthday, overspending, infidelity, or sabotaging the relationship in other harmful ways.

Fear of Rejection

We have met many couples in our practice who do not express their discomfort in a relationship because they fear rejection. For example, Nat knew Maureen had a quick and deliberate temper. He often felt as though he were "walking on egg shells" around her when he needed to bring up a potentially uncomfortable issue. Nat knew from experience that if he gave Maureen feedback about something she did or did not do, that Maureen would retaliate by enumerating all of his faults. Any attempt at a discussion would turn into a series of accusations, hurt feelings, and an awkward silence that lasted for a few days to more than a week. Nat believed this was how Maureen worked out her anger. He perceived that Maureen's aggressive and defensive behavior was related to Maureen's overcritical mother. He further concluded that Maureen was, in reality, reacting to issues she had with her mother when he and Maureen disagreed. So it was not a surprise when Nat suggested the couple come in for marital therapy. He was hopeful that he could improve his communication with his wife. Maureen reluctantly agreed, but once there, Nat shied away from expressing the intensity of his discontent in their marriage. He was deeply worried about the arguments and silences endured after leaving the sessions. He didn't want to be "punished" for what he might reveal in therapy.

Both Nat and Maureen were offered individual therapy to work on specific issues that stood in the way of success in marital therapy. By following this suggestion, Maureen made strides in developing insight into her interactions with Nat, and learned helpful anger management techniques and coping strategies for the unspoken resentment she felt toward her overcritical mother. She realized the control tactics she expressed in her marriage, by intimidating her husband from expressing his feelings and needs, were indeed similar to those she tolerated from her mother for many years.

Nat explored his intimidation of Maureen and realized this was related to his ongoing self-esteem issues that stemmed from having a super successful and attractive older brother with whom he was always negatively compared by his parents and former teachers.

Both Nat and Maureen were able to return to martial therapy with renewed awareness and freshly learned communication and conflict resolution skills that enabled them to relate to each other with respect and consideration. They were taught fair fighting techniques that aimed to allow each other to express their feelings in a constructive, rather than hurtful and negativistic manner. They learned to accept necessary feedback and to not respond with criticism and a litany of wrongs that were in the past and not related to the present discussion. This insight allowed them to realize that "tit for tat" fighting is unfair and leftover from their grade school days. They were taught what we regularly teach in our sessions: *"This is a marriage, not a competition!"*

THE IMPORTANCE OF A COUPLE'S SOCIAL HISTORY

As we meet with couples in therapy, we are always interested in their individual personal histories, as well as the history of their relationship. We want to know about their earliest experiences with their families or guardians. We inquire about their social histories with friends and significant others. We ask about their school and vocational experiences. This information is relevant since it helps us understand the basis for the couple's problematic interactions with each other. We may learn important historical facts that point to a pattern of unhappy relationships, discord with others, poor communication skills, anger management issues, and so forth.

As psychologists, we agree the original source of our interpersonal interactions and ultimately our relationships with our mates begin in our earliest experiences and continue throughout life. As keen observers, we witness and evaluate our interactions with each other and the interactions of our parents, grandparents, extended family members, neighbors, friends, teachers, and even the television programs we choose to watch. Our positive experiences in healthy family relationships provide us with a blueprint of expectations of future relationships. If we witness a family relationship in which respect, dignity, integrity, and love are in place, we will likely expect those characteristics in our relationships with others.

In contrast, if we are surrounded by dishonesty, anger, abuse, and instability, we may expect or be accustomed to those characteristics as well. We may have little hope that something better awaits us in future relationships unless we have the opportunity to witness positive relationships among others in our social setting. We may look to a best friend's parents for solace and a model for dignity and respect if it is lacking in our own family. We may set our behavior to that higher standard of interaction between others. Or we may continue to display the negative patterns of behavior that have historically surrounded us in our lives. We have found that many people who have been treated with disrespect or even abuse become tolerant of these behaviors. In therapy we noted that those patients are unaware that they tolerate more indignity in relationships than others who have been raised in emotionally healthier environments. This tolerance can set a pattern of accepting continued disrespect or abuse from future relationships. In therapy, these patterns of behaviors and unhealthy tolerance of abusive relationships are brought to the patients' attention. The goal is for them to be less accepting or tolerant of abuse or neglect from others in future relationships.

As psychologists, we believe we have a choice in how we respond to those in our environment despite our upbringing. Yet the impressions of our early social patterns are often imprinted and therefore hard to break unless we are aware of the inadequacy of these patterns and are taught how to make a change to a healthier lifestyle.

As children, we have all known those neighbors and classmates who fall into various categories: the class clown, the show-off, the liar, the athlete, the beauty queen, the popular kids, and the outcasts. As adults, the former class clown may always be the life of the party, and the one who is fun to be around. The show-off may always have to own the best house, the best car, designer clothes, and whatever else defines that person as superior to his peers. The liar may always be a stranger to the truth, and will consequently have trouble maintaining meaningful relationships in which honesty is coveted.

It is by these examples we illustrate the importance of our early experiences and how they influence what we perceive as our social selves or social personalities. We bring our pride, insecurities, level of self-esteem, and level of integrity into every relationship we enter.

When we meet someone special, we may try to conceal our flaws or inadequacies in hopes of making a good impression. In the "honeymoon" phase of a relationship, we may laugh heartily at stale jokes, tolerate loud music while driving, accept poor table manners, or a lack of cleanliness in an attempt to be accepted and ultimately loved for our good nature, patience, and tolerance of all things annoying. Indeed, if we do this we establish a high level of tolerance our partner may expect throughout the lifespan of the relationship. We have met so many patients who believe that if they appear to be the most giving, loving, and tolerant person their potential mate has ever met, then the person will be sure to marry them. They try to make their date see that they are matchless and therefore superior to all those that came before them. They stretch their powers of acceptance and patience to unhealthy limits to prevent loneliness and rejection. This is especially the case in relationships where there is a serious imbalance in power, such as where one person has a higher level of self-esteem, or a need and perhaps keener ability to control others in his environment than the other person, who is relinquishing any control that may appear to be available in their relationship.

In contrast, there are those who essentially "show their true selves" once they are feeling secure, or as some say, "once the ring is on the finger." This is the proverbial shocker of the "Jekyll and Hyde" bride or groom. We have all heard of the spouse who was "so sweet," "so kind," and "so loving" until the relationship developed into a comfortable pattern where lower standards of behavior became acceptable. Now the stamp of the relationship is created, and the patterns of behavior are defined and set, sometimes in stone. The challenge that awaits a spouse is to accept the "change" is possibly permanent (unless the spouse is willing to change to save the relationship) and to reconcile that he didn't really know his spouse before he married her. Or, the spouse can request a change and be either delighted at the positive response, or disappointed at being rejected.

The stamp of a given relationship appears certain when onlookers see the couple as one person. For example, a couple may be referred to as *Annieand-Mike* instead of Annie and Mike. The couple's name becomes one word. Their individual identities are blurred. That which is perceived as characteristic of one spouse may be assumed to be characteristic of the other.

We can well understand how difficult it is to change our marital stamp, or that which characterizes us as a couple. It is also clear that it is easier to change that stamp before it has solidified. We emphasize the importance of premarital therapy to correct imbalances in relationships, develop healthy boundaries, improve communication, learn to express needs in an effective manner, to respect each other, and cherish and nurture their marital bond.

THE CHALLENGES OF THERAPY

In marital therapy, we welcome the challenge to help those who are uncomfortable in a worn-out relationship. We challenge fundamentally happy and healthy couples to reach new levels of contentment. We support those who want to change and grow with their mate. We seek to find the core of compatibility that exists in the couples who meet with us. We try to uncover the initial spark that drew the couple together. We challenge the myth that change cannot be made in an established relationship. At the same time, we are realistic and know that patterns in a relationship are not made over night, and change takes time.

Dr. Katz has coined the phrase, "you cannot fight until you are ready to lose." This refers to warrior couples who realize they are ready to fight hard so they can better understand their spouses and improve their marital relationship. In the course of this fight, the couple may realize that although the fight was well fought, the battle cannot be won and their marriage cannot be saved. If this happens, they will have achieved a better understanding of why they are not compatible, how they have grown apart or have lost the love that previously sustained them. The warrior couple will try their best in marital therapy. They will be open to the opportunity this therapy affords them. They will not hold back, in hopes that they will be happily married once again!

Chapter Two

Assessment Phase

It is 9 a.m. and the telephone rings in our office. A potential patient is on the phone requesting an appointment for marital therapy. I say "potential" patient because in our experience, many patients don't follow through with their initial appointments. They schedule an appointment only to break it a few days later. Some don't even bother to call or come when scheduled. This may be due to their fear of facing tasks such as disclosing their intimate secrets to a stranger, hearing their mate's displeasure with them, feeling ridiculed in a public setting, having to relate painful incidents from both past and present events, admitting they have failed in some way, cost (since some insurance carriers do not cover marital therapy), the discomfort of stating they want to end the relationship in which they promised to "love and honor" their partner "till death do us part," or perhaps they have not as yet told their mate they were *finally* making the call that may either save or end their marriage.

In our experience, 80 percent of potential patients who call and immediately schedule an appointment keep them. Those who do not immediately schedule an appointment, but rather state "they will have to call back after talking to their spouse," usually do not follow through. They may get cold feet about making the leap to seek therapy. At other times the imminent crisis is over, so there is no need to make an appointment.

In our practice, we meet with couples who are dating, engaged, or married. We will often use the term "married" to describe our patient population, but all couples regardless of their marital status can effectively use the techniques we teach in our practice.

Evaluating the Presenting Problem

The assessment phase of our marital therapy program is when we evaluate the presenting problem and determine the course of therapy. Initially we meet with the couple together. This phase may take three or four sessions. We want to determine whether *both partners* want to work on the relationship. Naturally, if mutual interest is lacking no marital therapy can begin. Both have to commit to being interested in this journey for it to be successful.

We encourage each spouse to present the facts as he or she sees them. We discourage fighting, name calling, or harmful accusations. We encourage the couple to tell us "what went wrong" with their relationship. We attend to the discussion between the spouses and observe for differences in communication styles and opinion of the presenting problem. We also attend to their expressed embarrassment, hurt, and resentment toward each other.

As we continue with the couple in therapy, we assess for the potential of positive change within the marriage. We look for an indication of willingness of each to take responsibility for problem behaviors. We look for capability to compromise, to accommodate, and a willingness to agree or disagree without significant discord. Ultimately we assess if the marriage can be saved.

There are four questions we ask all couples who come in for marital therapy. A "yes" answer is required from both partners for marital therapy to proceed:

- Do you both want to save your relationship?
- Are you willing to work with each other to save it?
- Will you stop extramarital relationships during this process?
- Can you agree to turn over control to us for a period of time?

THE INITIAL PHASE OF THERAPY

During the initial phase of marital therapy, both partners are usually somewhat guarded. Many couples have difficulty discussing events from the past that are relevant to their current problems. The past we refer to can be from their earlier history before their relationship with each other, or relate to their history with each other. The former past events may relate to painful experiences from their upbringing, prior romantic relationships that have set faulty patterns of relating to others in a romantic relationship, and discussion of issues that have led to arguments in the past. The latter past issues may include unfulfilled hopes, plans, and dreams, lack of trust, poor communication skills, and the inability to openly discuss their most treasured goals for the future.

Our initial goal for marital therapy for all couples is improved trust and communication. Trust refers to two belief systems: (1) their spouse has been romantically faithful to them; (2) they can fully confide in their spouse without risk of being blamed, criticized, or insulted. Once both partners can fully trust each other, they are better able to communicate their thoughts and feelings. But for many couples, the inability to trust a spouse with their intimate feelings is what has fundamentally caused a breakdown in their communication. We continue to observe a tremendous fear of openness in the couples we treat. Essentially, this is the fear of taking a risk that will result in becoming vulnerable with their spouse. They are afraid that once they take that risk, their spouse has information that he or she can use against them somehow at some future date. In addition, they fear their spouse will tell others this important information, even though they have expressed it be kept confidential. In our sessions we encourage our couples to begin to trust one another. We encourage they take risks and begin to confide their thoughts and feelings with each other. Yet, we only encourage this type of risk taking if we believe both partners will respect the information that is shared and will not use it to hurt their spouse thereby causing further damage to their marital relationship. Realistically, we do not expect our couples to come into the first few sessions and easily share important issues they have been protecting for so long. As a happy couple, we model this respect in our sessions. We hope our couples learn from the lessons we demonstrate with each other, so they will learn to demonstrate this respect for each other. With this in mind, we gently approach the marital therapy process. We allow the couple to tell us information they are ready to share in an accepting and warm environment.

In our sessions, we ask about the history of their relationship. When we determine it is relevant, we also ask about their familial and friend histories. We ask questions about how they met, what activities they did together, what consisted of the *spark* that attracted one to the other. Most importantly, we want to know if the *spark* is still there.

In addition, we inquire what they do for a living, how they spend their leisure time, what they like to do for fun, and so forth. As we spend more time with the couple, we ask questions about their families, both immediate and extended. We want to know how holidays and birthdays are celebrated, what they do on vacations, we ask them to describe their relationships with their children and their pets. We want to know about their friends, and other aspects of their social life. We also want to know about their substance use or abuse, gambling, experience in pornography, infidelity, and other pertinent issues that may be affecting their marriage. After compiling this information, we have a clearer picture of the individuals who sit in our office. Of course in future sessions, we inquire about other delicate issues such as their sex life, financial concerns, employment history, and so forth. We try to make our inquiries comfortable for all concerned, and seek to have a better understanding of them as a couple and as individuals.

OUR ROLE AS THERAPISTS

Initially couples want to tell us the negative aspects of their relationship. Some may enter into a "he said, she said" interaction where angry feelings and blame are tossed back and forth. They look to us as referees in a game where one party is supposed to be the clear winner, and the other party is the loser. They put pressure on us to announce who is right and who is wrong. We naturally and gingerly avoid that trap as we delve further into learning about the circumstances that brought them into therapy. We are clear about our own roles with them. We help them to understand that our role is to provide therapy in a fair and objective manner. We are teachers in the delicate instruction of effective communication skills, conflict resolution, the stating of needs, the creation of realistic expectations, how to fight fair, and so much more. We repeat an important maxim that their *relationship is not a competition, it is a marriage.* It is an institution we respect, and in turn, we want them to learn to respect and protect it as well.

Sparks of Love

As previously stated, we encourage our couples to tell us what brought them together. We want to know how they met. Did they meet on a blind date; did they work together, were they classmates? We ask them to describe the initial sparks that ignited their dating relationship and prompted them into marriage. We look for evidence to see if those first sparks still exist. We ask the couple if those special feelings can be ignited once again. It is amazing how recalling pleasant memories can lead couples to relate happy and funny stories of when they were once hopeful and falling in love.

Strengths and Weaknesses in a Relationship

In our marital therapy, we explore both the strengths and weaknesses in a relationship. We hope to build on the strengths while we seek to diminish the weaknesses. After the first session, we ask our couples to complete a homework assignment. They are to independently write down the strengths and weaknesses in their relationship. Once the assignment is completed, we discuss it in future sessions.

Let's meet Jack and Macie who found difficulty with this task. Jack and Macie were like many couples who were still in love, but somehow lost track of what keeps them together as a couple. They argued about everything and were exhausted from the lengthy and loud exchanges they endured almost daily. Every discussion turned into a power struggle. Each partner was too threatened to back off or admit the other was correct. Obviously each had control issues that predated their marriage. Both were highly assertive, highly achieving individuals. In addition, they were both talented engineers who were employed in the same firm. Each competed for the same plum assignments and promotions. Their professional competitiveness seeped into their home life as well. They even took the assignment of naming their strengths and weakness as a competition to see who could name more of them.

At the end of four initial marital therapy sessions, Macie and Jack gained insight into how their professional relationship affected their marriage. They realized that their employers often pitted them against each other to achieve the best job performance. This realization prompted Macie and Jack to look for new positions in different engineering firms. Once they were no longer working for the same firm, they were able to focus on other issues that related to their need to compete with each other to win and to be right all of the time. They were also able to address their fear of appearing vulnerable and insecure in front of each other. Through the course of therapy, they learned the general elements of a strong relationship and those characteristics that weaken most, if not all, marriages. It is our effort throughout marital therapy to both model and teach those elements that strengthen a relationship, and those that weaken it, sometimes to the breaking point. We will now discuss some of the elements that strengthen a relationship and those that weaken it. A more in-depth discussion of these elements is provided in chapters 6 and 7.

Happy Couples and Successful Partners Share the Following Elements That Strengthen their Relationship:

- *Honesty in all interactions:* Each spouse tells the truth, no matter how difficult this can be at times. Both spouses are honest in their interactions with others, be they family, friends, neighbors, or co-workers. The task of honesty must include being respectful and having integrity. They must learn they can be honest while at the same time avoid being spiteful, hypercritical, and mean.
- *Trust in terms of loyalty and being able to keep matters confidential:* The spouses keep their issues to themselves and their marital therapists. They do not gossip negatively about each other to friends and family. The spouses and their children and pets are a family unit. They keep sacred each other's confidences and secrets. Both partners agree not to flirt or

romantically cheat on each other. If there is a desire to cheat, this is discussed together. They then must decide whether to separate, and/or discuss what is causing intense attraction outside of the marital union. If the attraction cannot be ignored, then a separation is considered.

- *Advocacy as it pertains to "having each other's back"*: There is an effort to realistically and appropriately fulfill each other's dreams, hopes, needs, and wishes as it pertains to their relationship: both partners are advocates for each other. They want to see their partner be happy and successful. They try to do whatever they can (within realistic and legal limits) to make each other happy.

- *Best friends:* The spouses in a happy couple are best friends. Each feels free to say what he or she thinks and feels in their relationship. They give each other feedback in a fair and respectful manner. Each spouse feels comfortable sharing his or her most treasured thoughts with his mate. This information is never shared with others or used in a vindictive way to hurt the other.

- *Integrity in all relationships:* Both spouses practice fair play in their inter- actions with everyone. They state what they believe, and their actions are consistent with their beliefs. They say as they do, and do as they say. They are trustworthy, dependable, and ethical in their dealings with each other and others in their lives.

- *Affectionate:* Both spouses enjoy being close to each other. They touch in both sensual and sexual ways. They are respectful of each other, and do not demand intimacy unless both spouses desire it. They can be playful as well as serious.

- *Marriage and family is their number one priority*: As stated, the married couple and their offspring are a family unit. They are loyal to this unit, and consider it first and foremost when making plans with others, keeping confidences, making monetary commitments, maintaining fidelity, and be- ing protective of their unit when others threaten to intrude in any way.

- *Understanding and respectful of feelings*: Both spouses attempt to know each very well. When one spouse is sad, mad, or happy, these emotions are discussed. A spouse may not agree or share these emotions, but he or she is willing to try to understand the reasons for these feelings. If a spouse is sad or mad, happy, or afraid, the other spouse is willing to openly discuss these feelings. He or she never negates these feelings by saying that the spouse should not feel this way. A spouse's feelings are considered to be important and of equal value to one's own feelings.

- *Availability during good and bad times*: Each spouse is there for the other during good times and bad. He is present to help out when his mate is sick. He is present to celebrate when his mate has met a goal or won a prize. He is clear that his family unit is his priority, and makes a concerted effort to prevent other people or events from interfering in family time together.

- *Realistic expectations of their spouse's actions and abilities*: Each spouse knows his mate's weak and strong points. He knows what his mate is capable of achieving, and what is not realistic. He does not expect his mate to achieve a level of competence in an area in which there is little aptitude or interest. He is available to bolster her strengths, and where possible, encourage her to decrease her weaknesses. He does not have expectations that have not been previously discussed with his mate. Expectations are discussed in advance. No one assumes the other will do a particular task before ascertaining it can and will occur.
- *Is present for all important occasions*: Each spouse makes a concerted effort to be present for all birthdays, anniversaries, holidays, and other celebrations. These special events are honored. They are never forgotten, overlooked, or deemed unimportant.
- *Fun is shared on a regular basis*: The spouses enjoy each other's company. They plan fun times together, even if it's a miserable day outdoors. They may take walks to get an ice cream cone, they enjoy holding hands while they walk on the beach, and light candles when they have dinner at home. Each day is considered special because they are together. For happy couples, this alone is worthy of a celebration.

Unhappy Couples and Ineffectual Partners Share These Elements:

- *Infidelity*: One or both spouses have romantic relationships outside of the marriage. Some individuals do not stop these affairs even when asked by their mate to do so. There are those couples who agree to have an *open* relationship that permits dating outside of the marriage. Most of the couples that we see have committed to a *closed* or traditional marriage where dating outside of the marriage is prohibited. Most spouses in closed marriages are particularly hurt when infidelity occurs. Yet many choose to stay with their partner and work through the issues that may have caused the infidelity to occur.
- *Constant arguing*: Some spouses get on each other's nerves. This is considered normal in the happiest of marriages. Most spouses get irritated from time to time, but for couples who are generally unhappy, every decision becomes a battleground for control. Some couples disagree to the point where they stop discussing issues for fear that another argument will ensue. They are agitated around each other, and often shout at each other to show their discontent and their effort to gain control of the presenting situation. Often the issue about which they are arguing is a mask for the deeper discontent that exists in the marriage. In therapy we attempt to identify the underlying discontent so it can be discussed and hopefully resolved.

- *Physical, verbal, and emotional abuse*: The spouses may physically assault each other. One or both spouses will engage in behavior that can lead to physical injury and sometimes to death. We strongly suggest any physical altercation between marital partners cease immediately. We consider it intolerable. We advise that the victim of the abuse strongly consider reporting the offending party to the police so further action can be taken. Often the victim is encouraged to live elsewhere to avoid further injury. There are other couples who do not physically harm one another but have developed a lifestyle of communication in which verbal abuse often occurs. Some individuals become verbally abusive when they are under stress, are agitated, not feeling well, and so forth. Others become emotionally abusive to their spouse by being unnecessarily critical, demeaning, insulting, or dismissive. We help our spouses to identify ways in which they are verbally and/or emotionally abusive. We remind them that by behaving in this manner, they only serve to hinder rather than promote effective communication. We remind these couples how to express their discontent in constructive and respectful ways. These methods are practiced in our sessions.
- *Inability to discuss matters large and small*: Every issue large and small becomes a fight for control. There are many disagreements, much anger, and an inability or unwillingness to resolve conflicts that exist between them. This often results in couples who are overwhelmed in life and with their relationship in general. Often there is a fear of having a disagreement with their spouse for fear of rejection or anger. In therapy we explore the reasons for the control issues we observe. We teach these couples how to express their views in a constructive manner. We further help them to identify which issues to explore together toward resolution, and which issues are best not to pinpoint as they may seem petty or inconsequential.
- *Absence from daily life together as well as from important activities*: This occurs when one or both spouses are not available to share in the running of the household. They ignore or postpone doing chores for which they have been assigned. They are not present to celebrate birthdays, go to PTA meetings, or accompany their mate if she has to have an operation, is giving birth, or is in trouble and needs her partner's support. This is a sign that a spouse is "running away" from the relationship and/or the responsibilities that exist in a functioning marriage. This lack of availability is sometimes due to a lack of maturity, a lack of interest in the relationship or their partner, or other issues that need to be discussed in therapy.
- *Dishonesty with each other as well as others*: There is an absence of truth and integrity. One or both spouses seek to get whatever they can in life, by whatever means are available. There is chronic lying, cheating, and poor excuses to mask their insincerity and their lack of caring and loyalty to their spouse. Dishonesty is often used to avoid the perceived conse-

quences that may occur if the truth is told. The result is a lack of trust in the spouse that has been dishonest. Sometimes the dishonest spouse is not believed even when he or she is telling the truth. The one who is dishonest must try to earn the trust of his or her partner by being honest in all interactions. This lack of trust is often most difficult to earn once it is lost.

- *Priorities lie outside of the family unit*: A spouse is more loyal to friends, neighbors, extended family members, or acquaintances than to his or her own immediate family. When this occurs, the offended spouse feels dismissed, betrayed, unloved, and unimportant. In therapy, priorities are discussed and identified. Measures are taken to elevate the family unit to the superior position that it deserves.

- *Inability to engage in give-and-take interactions*: One or both partners are selfish and self-centered. They use the word "I" instead of "we" in their interactions, because they do no think of themselves as a solid couple. They remain single people in a committed relationship. In therapy we teach this couple what constitutes a commitment, a marriage, and a partnership. These semi-committed individuals are taught to understand they are no longer alone in life, but rather have someone with whom to share the experiences that lie ahead with the person they have chosen as their mate.

- *Unwillingness to disclose thoughts and feelings*: There is absence of trust needed to share important thoughts and feelings. One or both partners remain distant and emotionally unavailable to the other. This lack of trust and/or emotional unavailability keeps spouses at a distance from one another. In therapy, the partners are encouraged to slowly take risks and open up to one another in a safe and accepting setting.

- *Gossip about marriage and family problems to others*: There is disloyalty in the immediate family. One or both spouses are dissatisfied with the other. They do not feel comfortable discussing their feelings with each other, so they go to outsiders for support. The gossip serves to erode trust between the partners. We teach it is important to keep key personal information within the family unit, and not to invite others, be it friends or family, into the marriage unit.

- *Spend more time with others outside of the marriage or family*: a spouse may consider the company of others to be more fulfilling and enjoyable, so the spouse spends much time away from his or her family members. The result is that the spouse and their children may feel rejected and abandoned, and may resent their spouse or parent for what is perceived to be emotional and physical distance. The issue here is again related to setting appropriate priorities within the family structure.

- *Emotional and physical coldness*: A mate may have difficulty getting close to others. He or she remains detached, unwilling to share feelings or be considerate of her family's needs and feelings. The spouse is uncomfortable with hugging, kissing, or other signs of affection. He or she does not display affection, nor accept affection from others. The result is a rejection of a partner's attempts to be giving and loving: A spouse may be cold and aloof when her partner wants to be affectionate. She or he may also reject other offerings such as gifts, compliments, or other attempts to be close. In therapy we explore the myriad of possible causes that can elicit this detachment. We discuss methods to achieve closeness in a relationship that has become somewhat estranged.

- *Incompatibility*: The partners may truly love each other but cannot live with each other without making each other crazy. They do not share the same core beliefs, ethical standards, personal habits, similar background, and other traits that contribute to compatibility. In the beginning of such a relationship, differences are often tolerated or overlooked. There may be a mistaken belief that "things will change once they are married." In therapy we do not attempt to change what lies at the core of each individual person. Instead, we emphasize the need to tolerate, respect, and accept these differences. When that is not possible, a separation and or divorce may occur.

Our couples often come up with other behaviors that may or may not benefit their marriage or relationship. The ones listed above represent those that are commonly mentioned in our sessions, but are certainly not representative of all types of weaknesses that may exist in relationships. In therapy we discuss each strength and weakness we encounter. We attempt to reinforce the strengths, while we chip away at those elements that are eroding the marriage.

GROUND RULES

As we begin to analyze the couple's strengths and weaknesses, we assign initial mandatory ground rules that the couple must follow outside of the therapy session. We have found these ground rules are essential to successful marital therapy. The ground rules represent a set of healthy boundaries for couples who tend to "cross the line" in their relationships with each other. These ground rules include the following:

- *No extramarital affairs.* It is impossible to have successful marital therapy if one or both partners are romantically involved with others.
- *No physical or verbal abuse.* Successful marital therapy requires mutual respect for the safety and integrity of both marital partners.

- *No destructive accusations of each other are allowed outside of the marital therapy session.* In our sessions we will discuss how to express discontent in a constructive manner.
- *No arguments.* Instead, the couple is asked to write down their issues and bring the written material to our sessions for discussion.
- *No discussion of potential conflict areas.* These too will be discussed in ongoing therapy sessions.

As stated previously in this chapter, we initially meet with a couple for three to four sessions, and then determine if they can continue meeting as a couple, or if they need individual sessions to discuss existing personal issues that are preventing progress in the marital therapy sessions.

We discussed Macie and Jack earlier in this chapter. I met with Jack in individual therapy while my husband met with Macie. Each had six individual sessions before they returned to marital therapy. We felt both had individual issues that needed further exploration. We learned that Macie was one of six children, and was the only girl in the family. She had always competed with her brothers for her parents' attention, and found herself unable to "back down" or relent in her efforts for fear her family would dismiss her or call her "only a girl," "weak," or "not as good as the boys." Apparently these were phrases that were often used by her family members to "encourage her to be the best she can be." At work and in her marriage to Jack, she was relentless in her efforts to *prove* herself. She automatically responded to Jack as if he were another one of her brothers. He became a competitor for approval and someone to beat at all costs. In the course of therapy, Macie was able to see Jack as a loving husband, and someone to join with her rather than oppose her in creating and approaching goals for their future. She was able to see him as less of a threat and more as a marital partner. She no longer felt alone in her attempts to fight her battles in life.

Jack was the youngest of three children. His older sister, Janet, was the "successful one." She always had the best grades, got into the best college, and so forth. When he got involved with Macie, he soon recognized her need to compete with him. This brought back all of his feelings of being inferior to Janet, which prompted him to step up and try his best to not be bested again. Individual therapy helped him to gain insight into his feelings about his parents and their favoritism toward Janet. He was better able to gain insight into these feelings and not attribute them to his wife.

What Went Wrong

Once back in marital therapy, couples like Macie and Jack have a fresh perspective of the issues that challenge their marriage. They are better able to look at "what went wrong" in their relationship without reverting back and repeating negative behaviors that stem from the lingering burdens of their past.

When we consider "what went wrong" in a given relationship, we are faced with a myriad of possible factors. We realize that "what went wrong" can happen at any time in a relationship. It can happen while the couple is dating, engaged, or married. We will now explore *what went wrong* with Jane and Ben.

Jane was thirty-nine years old when she met Ben. Jane had always been expected to marry. Her parents wanted her to be *happy* and believed a young woman could not be happy without a husband and children. Jane dated quite a bit, but never found "the right one." Her parents continued to pressure her by reminding her that she "had very few, if any fertile years left." Indeed, this pressure increased with each wedding and baby shower she attended. Jane had few single friends left and, in fact, one of her friends was already a grandmother!

Unhappy with her career course, Jane decided to make a change for the better. She began this venture by going to night school. In her Wednesday evening class she met Ben, a single forty-two-year-old who was interested in expanding his professional skills. Jane and Ben became study partners, and then became an engaged couple within five months of their first night school class together. Jane's parents and friends were thrilled. There was endless discussion of flowers, party favors, a band, and of course, the dress!

At first Jane was caught up in the excitement of an impending marriage, but it wasn't long before she found herself unable to sleep. She lost weight, and snapped at Ben who was nothing but supportive and easy going. Jane called for a therapy session after she had an "anxiety attack" at work.

Through the course of therapy we determined *what went wrong*. We learned Jane was happy being single. The pressure to marry came from outside of herself, specifically from persons in her life. In addition, she felt she really didn't know Ben well enough to start a marriage with him. Jane ended the engagement, and returned to a life where she felt empowered to set priorities for herself. Once this was accomplished, she was able to sleep through the night once again. With the pressure of a wedding and a marriage off the calendar, Jane dated lots of interesting men and is getting to know herself better, especially what she is looking for in a potential mate.

A False Sense of Intimacy

Ben was different. He wanted to date, get married, and raise a family. He was ready and willing to begin a serious relationship. This led him to read an article about the benefits of online dating. He was excited to meet someone new and quickly developed a computer dating relationship with Angela. During the course of their conversations, they shared personal details from their childhood, adolescent years as well as their hopes and dreams, and their intimate fantasies. When they finally met, they "fell in love" and married within a month.

Ben called our office after only two months of marriage. He described his relationship as "failing" and didn't know why this was happening. He reported they were best of friends over the internet, but now Ben believed they didn't know each other at all. He felt Angela misrepresented herself to him, and he did not like what he described as the "New Angela." "What went wrong" in Ben and Angela's relationship was a false sense of intimacy. What they originally determined to be love and friendship in a safe cyberspace relationship became nothing less than two strangers who shared a house together.

Our society values family and togetherness. We are in favor of marriage, and put much pressure on those who do not meet this societal standard. We also put much pressure on couples to stay together despite incompatible styles of communicating, different coping skills and strategies, different life goals, and so forth. So when we meet with a new couple in therapy, we immediately begin to assess "what went wrong." We determine if the wrongs in a given relationship can be made right or if they are unable to be fixed.

Indeed, as we learned from Jane, many couples mention that "what went wrong" is related to outside influences on their relationship. Whether it be from family pressures, job stressors, financial burdens, health factors, or a loss of friendship within the relationship, we must assess each causal factor to determine how to improve the relationship, or if it can be saved.

In upcoming chapters we will discuss how to increase effective two-way communication, how to appropriately express needs so a marital partner can hear and appreciate them, how to create and meet mutual goals, and how to revive romance that lies smoldering under all the "what went wrongs" in a given relationship. We help the couples we meet to understand that as we revive the feelings of love, and romance in a given relationship, it is impossible to go back to how if was weeks, month, or years ago. Times and people change. The gallons of water under the bridge of a failing relationship cannot be purified. A couple in their forties cannot return and recapture how life was when they were in their twenties. So our emphasis is to start fresh with a new love, a new understanding, a new appreciation of each other. This begins by learning the important effective relationship skills that we discuss in the next chapters.

Chapter Three

Learning the Basic Skills of Listening and Understanding

101

You cannot pick up a book or article on how to improve a relationship without reading about *communication*. It may seem to some that this word or concept is too simplistic and overused, but in our opinion, it is not emphasized or used enough. It is a very broad term that means different things to different people. There are jokes about poor communication between couples. The standard line is "My wife (or husband) doesn't understand me." I saw a tee shirt recently with the following inscription: "My wife complains I don't listen to her. What did she say?" Even dogs are getting into the act with bumper stickers and tee shirts that state, "What part of *WOOF* don't you understand?"

Here's a joke that also points to our use of comedy regarding relationships with poor communication skills: *A woman walks into a lawyer's office and says she wants a divorce from her husband of thirty years. The lawyer asks, "Why?" and the woman says, "What do you mean?" So the lawyer says, "Do you have any grounds for a divorce?" The woman replies, "What grounds, we live in an apartment." The lawyer asks, "Do you have a grudge with your husband?" The woman replies, "No, he is too cheap to have a garage; we park on the street." The lawyer asks, "Does he ever beat you up?" The woman replies, "No, the lazy bum sleeps til noon, and I get up at 6 a.m." Finally the lawyer says, "What is the problem?" And the woman replies, "We don't communicate!"*

Comedians have fun joking about poor communication skills, but for those who have these problems, it's no fun at all! In this book, we discuss various exercises and techniques that we use to help our patients improve their communication skills. We encourage our patients to practice these skills both in and out of our sessions until they are confident that communication is no longer a problem area in their relationship.

COMMUNICATION STYLES

We encounter many styles of communication in our practice. Here is a description of a few we encounter the most.

The Sharer

These individuals enjoy sharing news about their day, what they heard on TV, experiences they had at the bank, dry cleaner, and so forth. They tend to be open about their feelings and thoughts. Sometimes they need to censor their inner lives more often, as they appear to be an open book with everyone, even those who may not be interested in every detail of their lives. The *sharer* prefers to relate to others who are also open about their lives. They feel shut out, ignored, or avoided by those who are what we call the *mummers*.

The Mummer

These individuals have the philosophy "mums the word." They are often private people who are not apt to share much about themselves. Many of these people believe much of what they do or experience is not particularly noteworthy. Some believe their experiences are "no one's business." When asked about their day, how they feel about certain issues, and so forth, they tend to respond by giving short answers. They may be perceived as guarded, secretive, or evasive by others. Quite often they have trust issues that prevent them from opening up and sharing their thoughts and feelings. The *mummers* are frustrating companions for the *sharers*.

The Inquisitor

These individuals like to learn information about others. They love to get details from others about their everyday lives. They may ask their spouse lots of questions about their day, their plans, why they behave as they do, how they feel about certain things, and so on. They may be perceived as intrusive by the *mummers* who tend not to share as readily as the *inquisitor* would prefer. In contrast, they may also be perceived as being fully interested in those persons in their lives. The *sharer* would in general be more comfortable with the *inquisitor* in terms of communication-style, providing the *inquisitor* is also willing to be a *sharer*.

The Partial Responder

These individuals are closer in nature to the *sharer,* but tend to leave out pertinent information the *sharer* and *inquisitor* find important. Their tendency to be selective in what they reveal makes them appear suspicious or secretive. They seem as though they have something to hide. There may be a bumpy road ahead for this individual if their spouse learns the information they have opted to leave out of conversations was important to discuss. Indeed the *sharer* and *inquisitor* find these individuals frustrating to have as close friends or spouses. The *mummer* may find their communications style more compatible, but equally frustrating if important information consistently fails to be revealed to them.

The Forgetter

These individuals tend to forget to tell their spouse pertinent information that may be deemed necessary to discuss. They may get distracted, busy, or simply put, have a poor memory. It is difficult to determine if they have honestly forgotten the information that needs to be shared, or if they have chosen to "forget" to reveal these items. The *sharer* or *inquisitor* find them frustrating as they have to be constantly reminded to keep track of important events, interesting facts, and sensitive conversations with others. The *partial responder* or *mummer* understand them better than the *sharer* or *inquisitor.*

The Manipulator

Here is a challenging individual who controls or manipulates others from having open and honest conversations. This individual loses his or her temper or gets a negativistic attitude when others want to talk to them about something important. Their behavior and attitude intimidates others from speaking up. Consequently open communication shuts down. This failure to communicate causes much distance in marital relationships. This individual is a challenge for all the other types of communication style individuals we have discussed thus far.

Regardless of a person's style of communicating, our goal is to help bridge gaps that exist due to difference in styles of communication, and lack of understanding and insight into how to more adequately relate to others.

CLARIFY COMMUNICATION

A technique we use in our sessions is called "clarify communication." One spouse discusses a neutral topic that he or she has perhaps read about in the newspaper, or has heard or seen while watching television. The initial discussion lasts for three to five minutes. We encourage that the chosen topic be neutral, unrelated to their relationship, and not contain sensitive or potentially volatile information. It could be a review of a movie, the results of a ballgame, or a joke heard at work. The marital partner who was listening to the information states what she or he has heard and is encouraged to be factual. The spouse who made the initial statement gives their spouse feedback regarding whether he or she was heard correctly. Restatements of the original comment are made until the couple feels certain it was sufficiently understood.

When we use *clarify communication* as a tool designed to improve communication, our goal is to make clear or *clarify* all statements that have the potential to be either misunderstood, or not heard at all. Another goal of this exercise is to improve listening skills and help each spouse feel more comfortable giving feedback to each other regarding their listening and communication skills.

After our couples achieve comfort with this exercise, they may move on to discuss more pertinent and sensitive topics of concern to them. Here is an example of this exercise:

Wife: *"I get nervous when I am around your mother."*

Husband's faulty interpretation: *"You never liked my mother!"*

Wife's restatement: *"I never said I don't like your mother. I think she is a nice woman, but she makes me nervous whenever I am around her."*

Husband's correct interpretation: *"You think my mother is a nice woman, but you feel nervous around her."*

Husband's correct following statement: *"Could you tell me more about what causes you to be nervous when you are around my mother?"*

In the husband's faulty interpretation, he wrongly accuses his wife of disliking his mother. This was both a false assumption and a wrong conclusion. In this case the husband acted in a defensive manner and essentially disregarded his wife's first statement. He was not sensitive to his wife's feelings about why she is nervous around his mother. His initial statement had the potential to cause an argument that could have derailed the conversation. In response, the wife could have become hurt or angry if she felt her husband did not demonstrate appropriate concern for why she is nervous around his mother.

In later statements, the husband voiced an appropriate interpretation of his wife's initial statement, and showed concern and interest in her feelings by asking for more information on this delicate subject.

Understanding

Communication and understanding go hand in hand. One marital partner can carefully and clearly state what is on his or her mind, but if her partner doesn't *understand* her, then successful communication simply does not occur. Successful understanding requires certain elements be in place. For example, the words themselves must be understood. The use of vocabulary is important. If one partner uses words or colloquial expressions that the other partner doesn't know, then effective communication does not occur. After all, no one wants to use a dictionary while speaking to his or her significant other. To purposely use vocabulary words or expressions that a spouse does not understand is a deliberate attempt to "put them down" and/or leave them out of the conversation.

This reminds me of the *I Love Lucy* show, when the character Ricky spoke in Spanish whenever he was annoyed or exasperated by his wife, Lucy. The audience related to Lucy's confused expressions when Ricky rattled off a sentence in Spanish indicating he was upset. Of course Lucy could tell her husband was unhappy by his facial expression and raised voice, but the exact reason for the unhappiness eluded her.

When one does not understand the words a spouse uses to express her feelings, the likely result is the spouse will eventually tune her out, or will simply stop listening. So when she complains her spouse doesn't *listen* to her, she's right!

True understanding that our happy couples demonstrate requires the use of clear concepts to express a thought or feeling. If a marital partner speaks using metaphors or other indirect or abstract statements, chances are a misunderstanding will occur. At times our patients will use abstract terminology or unique expressions to avoid clearly explaining their thoughts and feelings. This is a way for them to avoid stating directly what they think or feel about a particular topic. This can occur for a variety of reasons. One reason is the spouse is trying to avoid an argument with his spouse. Another reason may be to avoid receiving a negative or judgmental response from his spouse.

Simply stated, for understanding to take place and effective communication to occur we must clearly state exactly what we think and feel about an issue. To meet this goal, we ask our couples to restate comments that are esoteric, or contain metaphors, or vocabulary that is difficult to understand.

In contrast, we encourage our couples to make clear and concise statements. Then we check in with our couples to make sure they agree the statements used were clearly understood by both parties involved in the conversation.

For Example:

Wife: *"My husband is a typical man who doesn't think before he acts."*

Husband: *"What are you complaining about now? All she does is complain, complain, and complain some more!"*

Wife: *"You acted like a typical man when you yelled at the phone company about our incorrect phone bill."*

Husband: *"You acted like a typical wife who gave the problem to me to handle; I'm sick of that!"*

Wife: *I guess I do expect you to handle the uncomfortable issues we encounter, and then I get mad at you for being assertive. I'm jealous that I have trouble confronting people and you do it so easily. But don't say it's because I'm a woman; I know lots of assertive women. I think you're sexist and I don't like that, so cut it out!*

Husband: *"Whoops, I guess my statement was sexist and out of hand, but so was saying that I am a typical man! Maybe we could talk about ways you could be more assertive so I don't always have to handle the difficult stuff."*

Here the husband and wife attempted to work out their differences by recognizing they use meaningless clichés to express their discontent with each other. When expressing discontent about a partner's behavior, it is vitally important to be specific, and provide relevant examples to prove a point. General statements such as "she is a typical woman" or "he's an annoying husband" are meaningless, derogatory, and only causes more anger and dissention between the couple. Clearly, general statements of this sort destroy instead of encourage healthy communication.

When we refer to healthy communication, we refer to the use of clear words and concepts, as well as the expression of honest and directly stated thoughts and feelings. Of course before thoughts and feelings can be clearly stated, one must be able to understand both how one feels and the reasons why one really feels a certain way. Sometimes a spouse will express discontent, but is not sure why he or she feels that way. They have not given themselves time to reflect on these feelings before expressing them. They may tell a spouse they are angry with them, but may not really know why they are angry, or if the word *angry* truly describes their thoughts and feelings. The anger they express may be a mask for hurt feelings, being disappointed, or feelings of insecurity.

We always tell our couples to reflect on their thoughts, feelings, and reactions before they express them to their spouse. We encourage them to express their true feelings, rather than respond with spontaneous reactions to what they perceive as frustrating or upsetting events.

We help our patients to be consciously aware of incidents when they use inaccurate or hurtful words to mask intense feelings that they are uncomfortable expressing. We teach them to be respectful of each other, and to not be insulting or demeaning when they try to express their feelings. We teach them to avoid hiding behind their false concepts or hurtful words when they are insecure about how they will be received by their mate if they are truly honest about their thoughts and feelings. We teach our couples how to take risks and be honest about stating their feelings, even when they fear an unwanted reaction such as rejection or anger. We help our couples understand that to be successfully understood in a close relationship, one must be able to convey intimate thoughts and feelings so each spouse knows exactly how the other spouse feels and thinks about the subject being discussed.

As stated earlier in this chapter, the use of understandable vocabulary words and statements that describe thoughts and feelings help couples achieve a better understanding of each other. This results in more effective communication in their relationship. When we observe a lapse in communication, we ask a spouse to repeat or reword her ideas until they are presented in a clear and understandable manner.

"I" Statements

Effective communication requires owning one's thoughts and feelings. When we express a thought or feeling, we must use *I* statements to convey how we think or feel. It is vitally important to say *I feel*, or *I think*, when speaking to others, regardless of the nature of the relationship. The use of *I* statements is useful in romantic relationships, as well as in interactions at work, with family members, in conversations with friends, neighbors, and so forth. When using the word *I,* the speaker takes responsibility for his or her thoughts and feelings, and is not blaming them on someone else.

Many couples who have difficulty using effective communication skills use the term *you* instead of *I*. Consider this example of a patient who was annoyed with the way her boyfriend paid attention to her sister: "You always pay lots of attention to my sister when you are with my family." When asked to clarify her thoughts by rewording her statement by using the word *I,* she stated, "I feel hurt that you spend so much time with my sister at family gatherings. I worry you are attracted to her." The second statement took courage, but was much more direct and honest. It allowed her boyfriend to consider and comment on her concern without feeling attacked.

Effective communication skills require that we take responsibility for how we think and feel. We must avoid transferring these thoughts and feelings onto someone else.

Speaking to Each Other

During our sessions, we encourage our couples to speak directly to one another. This requires that they look at each other when speaking. We discourage our couples from looking at us when they are talking about or to their spouse. We want them to make eye contact, and speak clearly to one another. In addition, we encourage them to stay calm when expressing their thoughts and feelings. We instruct them to avoid shouting or cursing at each other.

We know there are times when couples get angry and shout at one another. Nevertheless, we have found that people tend to shout because they don't feel like they are being heard. It is human nature that when one feels like he is not being heard, he becomes frustrated and sometimes angry. When a person raises her voice when she is frustrated and angry, she hopes her partner will better hear or understand her. We remind our couples that a raised voice does not insure they will be heard. Rather, a raised voice from one spouse prompts a raised voice from the other in return. When we shout at our mate, an employee, or a neighbor, we are essentially pushing them away. We are rejecting them. We are making them feel uncomfortable. At times we frighten them. When someone shouts at us, the consequence is that we tend to hear the volume and intensity of the voice more than the words being spoken. As stated earlier in this chapter, we teach our couples effective communication skills and recommend that to be correctly heard one should try restating a comment using clear concepts, reasonable vocabulary, as well as *I* statements, and a neutral tone of voice.

Communication Robbers

In today's mode of communication, we have found texting, email, and Facebook are the norm. Many of our patients use texting or email as their way to speak to each other. They tend to feel more courageous using the written word. They can say things in a text they would never say in person or over the telephone. By using writing rather than speaking, miscommunication can and often occurs. When we speak to one another, especially in person, we hear voice inflection and see body language and facial expression. This gives us so much more information than the written word can ever achieve. That is why we encourage our patients to speak to each other rather than use text or email to effectively communicate, especially when they have something important to say.

The use of Facebook to communicate is very popular. Our patients post notes and pictures that describe their activities, preferences, and even information about their relationships. They often announce their dating/marital status on Facebook. Yet this has posed a problem for some of our patients who have chosen to post too much of their personal lives on their sites. Misunderstandings and hurt feelings often occur when our patients visit sites of friends and family. They may see photos of what appears to be close friendships and romantic relationships that cause jealousy, hurt, and anger. We continue to encourage our patients to be less open on their sites and to cease from essentially spying on or stalking their significant others in order to purposely find out more information about the personal lives of their friends and lovers. We prefer that our patients learn about each other through face-to-face conversation rather than through internet sites. In marital therapy we help our patients to better know their partners by structured means such as the completions of lists we prepare for them.

USING LISTS IN THERAPY

We are careful to avoid hot or sensitive topics early in the therapeutic relationship. We are getting to know the couple and are observing their mode of communication. We want them to feel comfortable with us and to learn to feel comfortable with each other. As we progress in therapy, we have noticed our couples try to change the subject or steer away from important discussion topics. This generally occurs to avoid the important or difficult issues we are attempting to resolve. Nevertheless, we encourage our couples to stay on the topic being discussed. We then explore reasons for resistance to discuss issues that are being addressed in therapy.

Our mode of therapy requires the completion of homework assignments that provide the couple with continued practice in talking to one another. We ask our couples to bring completed homework assignments into the sessions for discussion. Naturally we discuss reasons for assignments that are not completed on time. We ask our couples not to discuss their homework assignments with each other unless the assignment requires they do their homework together.

Our first assignment is to be completed before the second therapy session. Each spouse is asked to make a list of the things *they want to change about themselves* so they can improve their relationship. They are also asked to complete a list of the things *they want their spouse to change* as well. These two lists usually contain items such as these:

- I need to be a better listener when talking to my spouse.
- I want my partner to be more understanding.
- I need to help with dinner more often.
- I want my partner to do more chores around the house.
- I need to stop working on the weekends, so we can have more time together.
- I want my partner to be less controlling.
- I need to stop complaining about everything.
- I want my spouse to spend more time with me.
- I want to spend less time with my friends and more time with my spouse.
- I want my partner to play with the children.
- I want my partner to be honest with me

We find that creating lists helps the couple structure their thoughts about their relationship. This structure is important, because it creates healthy boundaries when discussing thoughts and feelings that are sensitive and difficult to express. Plus it helps the couple to be concise about their issues, and it prevents lengthy directionless diatribes about what is wrong with the relationship.

List of Regrets

One of the lists we want our couples to prepare is two *lists of regrets* they have about their marriage. The regrets are those areas in life they wish were different. Examples can include having children earlier in life, getting a better education, forgetting a birthday or anniversary, putting good effort into a bad job, and so forth. Another list includes naming five things each spouse regrets regarding his or her own behavior toward their spouse. Examples can include the following: including my spouse with my family when we got together for birthdays and such, being honest, being faithful to our vows, and so forth. As we review these lists in therapy, we inquire about ways in which the relationship suffered as a result of the regrets. We ask our couples to determine if any of the regrets can be "fixed," or is it too late to change what now constitutes a regret. Naturally if changes can be made, then the couple is encouraged to make the effort to do so. If changes cannot be made to rectify a situation, then the couple is asked to cease from dwelling on the regret, and allow it to remain in the past. We further encourage our couples to try to recover from the guilt they have for doing or not doing certain behaviors for which they feel regret. They are asked to genuinely apologize to one another for past transgressions. They are also asked to forgive themselves, which often is the hardest task of all! Finally, our couples are asked to make a promise to themselves and to each other that when or if a similar situation arises in the future, they will not make the same mistake they now currently regret.

After preparing their lists, the couple is asked to not share them with each other prior to the next therapy session. At the start of our next session, we collect the lists and carefully review them. If the lists are congruent, we review them with the couple at the start of the therapy session. If the lists are vastly different, we put them aside to be discussed when better communication between the couple is obtained.

We assign the creation of other lists during the course of our weekly therapy sessions.

These lists include:

- *Name five things you want to change about yourself.* This list can include: Improve my hygiene, stop smoking, be a better cook.
- *Name five things you want to change or improve about your spouse/ partner.* This may include: Losing weight, being more honest, and spending more time with the children.
- *Name five things you think your spouse/ partner would like to change or improve about him or herself.* This may include: Getting a better job, following a healthier diet, or drinking less alcohol after work.
- *Name five things that are good about the relationship.* This list may include: We have fun together, we share similar values, or we love each other.
- *Name five bad things about the relationship.* This list may include: We fight all the time, we don't make time for each other, or we are tired of each other.
- *Name five things that you like about your spouse/ partner.* This list may include: A good sense of humor, nice build, or makes friends easily.
- *Name five things you do not like about your spouse/ partner.* This list may include: A bad temper, poor relationship with family members, or is angry most of the time.
- *Name five things your spouse/ partner could do to help the relationship.* This list may include: Be more loving and affectionate, help with the chores, or be honest more often.
- *Name five things you can do for your spouse/ partner to help the relationship.* This list may include: Be home on time from work, help with dinner preparation, spend less time with friends on weekends.

- *Name five things I regret about my behavior toward my spouse/ partner.* This list may include: Not being considerate of his feelings, not taking his side in family battles, or yelling at him in front of the children.
- *Name five things I can do to change my regrets into hopes for the future.* This list can include: Be less critical of others, spend more time with loved ones, or keep the promises I make.
- *Name five things I plan to do in the coming year that will improve our relationship.* This list can include: Save more money from each paycheck, be there for important occasions, or take a course that will improve my chance for a promotion at work.

When all of the lists are completed, we check to see if responses to the lists correspond between partners. We look for a shared perception of what is going well and what needs to be improved in their relationship. As our couples advance their communication skills, they move down from one list to the next. Each list is thoroughly discussed. Progression to the next list requires the couple to completely resolve all of the issues that have been identified in the preceding list. We have found the creation and discussion of these lists helps the couple focus on the important issues in their relationship, gives them an opportunity to vent their frustrations in a thoughtful and concise manner, and helps them build more effective communication and understanding skills, and serves to uncover additional important topic areas that may spontaneously arise during our discussions.

As we progress in our marital or relationship therapy sessions, we help our couples to clearly interpret the issues each brings to the sessions. We teach them how to effectively communicate so they can better understand each other. We encourage them to use vocabulary they both can interpret. We ask them to repeat each other's statements to insure greater understanding and communication. We review the correct use of *I* statements, and encourage them to establish eye contact when speaking to each other. Above all, we want them to practice respect for each other, and avoid making insulting or negative remarks that can cause further distance between them. We are preparing them for more advanced communication skills that they will learn in future sessions.

Chapter Four

Learning Effective Communication Skills

102

The couples we have in therapy are encouraged to practice daily the communication skills they are taught in our sessions. By going to therapy and practicing these skills at home our patients notice an enhancement in the quality of their relationships.

Every couple has conflicts. Some couples have more conflicts than others. Some conflicts are minor and are easily or quickly resolved. Others are more serious and longstanding. There are couples who argue about their finances, demanding in-laws, problems with their children, and home repairs. Many spouses have job pressures they bring home to their families. Insecurities and anger at supervisors or co-workers may be manifested in arguments with a mate or with children.

Spouses who are in the "sandwich generation" may have stressful issues with both taking time to care for ailing and aging parents, while also caring for their own children who need much of their time and patience. Other spouses argue over current or former lovers, past disappointments, or feelings of rejection or loneliness.

When we meet with a couple, we determine the exact source of their conflicts. We determine if the conflicts are related to unresolved issues from the past, or are due to recent or ongoing events. We inquire about the exact nature of the conflicts or arguments so we can determine what happened to cause a marital partner to be hurt or angry. We ask our patients to have integrity and take responsibility for their actions that have been disruptive to their relationship. We discuss maladaptive coping techniques the couple has used to deal with their conflicts. We want to know if they have been open and honest about the problems they are having, or if one or both spouses have quietly dismissed them as if they do not exist, or have purposely hidden them to avoid arguments or other forms of conflict. After we have learned how a couple deals with their conflicts, we introduce them to effective techniques they can use to solve the conflicts they are currently addressing.

CONFLICT RESOLUTION

In order for our couples to successfully discuss the issues that concern them, they must also be able to resolve their differences in an effective manner. We refer to this process as *conflict resolution*. Our goals for discussing conflict areas are to relieve tension, remove uncomfortable negative emotions such as anger and fear, and create a calm "businesslike" discussion for the common good of the relationship. We recommend that only one conflict is discussed at a time, and that the couple focus all of their attention to the following exercise:

Person A (which could be a girlfriend, spouse, or fiancé) states he or she wishes to discuss a particular topic with Person B. In the beginning, we prefer the topic be fairly neutral so the couple can practice resolving conflicts that are not very important to them. Person A tells Person B the main subject of the discussion topic or conflict by using very few words. They may say they wish to discuss finances, or their wedding plans, a family member, and so forth.

Person A gives Person B a choice to discuss the topic in forty-five or ninety minutes.

Person B chooses when to proceed with the discussion, in either forty-five or ninety minutes.

When the discussion takes place, the couple is seated at a table with a notebook and pen. The notebook becomes their *Conflict Resolution Notebook*, and will be used for all future discussion of conflict areas. The *Conflict Resolution Notebook* will be further discussed in chapter 11.

There are no distractions or the consumption of alcohol or street drugs allowed during this discussion. This is the recommended process for successful conflict resolution:

Person A describes the nature of the conflict in a clear and respectful manner. After Person A finishes describing the conflict in five minutes or less, Person B repeats what Person A just said. Person A then states whether Person B correctly or incorrectly understood the opening statement.

At this time, Person A may restate the original statement, allowing Person B to repeat what was said. When Person A feels Person B correctly heard the statement, then the discussion moves to the *conflict resolution phase*.

In the *conflict resolution phase*, Person A writes down both the subject of the conflict and a recommendation on how to resolve it. Person B reads what Person A wrote and has a choice to accept it or to write a different resolution. A discussion of possible resolutions takes place. Once a mutual resolution is agreed upon, it is written in the *Conflict Resolution Notebook*. Then the agreement is signed and dated by both persons.

If the same or similar conflict arises in the future, the couple can refer to the *Conflict Resolution Notebook* to determine how to solve it. They need not argue about the same issue at a later date. The *Conflict Resolution Notebook* becomes an invaluable resource. It helps the couple resolve many if not all of their conflict areas. It reminds them of the successful work they accomplished by being able to calmly and effectively discuss the topics that were once impossible to approach. For this reason, we recommend the *Conflict Resolution Notebook* be kept in a central and safe location where it cannot be lost, misplaced, or ruined.

Conversational Topic Areas

We ask our couples to practice communication exercises on a daily basis. As previously stated, in the beginning of therapy we encourage our couples to practice on "cold topic" areas. Once they are more adept at discussing these topics, they can advance to "medium" and then to "hot" topic areas.

Hot topics include those that brought the couple into therapy. In the past, discussion of these topics usually resulted in an argument that remained unresolved. The couple has not been able to arrive at workable solutions to these topics. Examples of *hot topics* from our practice include physical, verbal, and/or emotional abuse; substance abuse; marital infidelity; chronic dishonesty; issues related to intimacy; extreme spending habits; betrayal; lack of respect; and previous relationships.

Medium topics include those that remain difficult to discuss in a calm fashion, but do not evoke the same intense reactions as the hot topics described above. Examples of medium topics from our practice include completion of chores or responsibilities, general financial problems, issues related to children, career concerns, problems concerning parents and extended family members, ongoing disappointment in various aspects of the relationship, and failure to agree on various decisions regarding their present and future activities.

Cold topics are irritating to the couple, but the couple has found a way to cope with them so they are not considered a primary or secondary influence on their relationship. Examples of cold topics from our practice include annoying friends or anyone who has a toxic effect on the relationship, personal hygiene differences, annoying habits that can grate on one's nerves, household and car repairs, and interference from outside obligations.

We must add that *cold topics* for one couple may be *hot topics* for another. Each couple is considered an individual entity that has its own special way of interpreting conflict areas. In addition, issues considered cold, medium, or less important topic areas may become medium or hot if they are not dealt with in a timely and effective manner.

Daily Communication Exercise

We ask our couples to set aside twenty minutes a day to practice a daily communication exercise. The couple must agree to not discuss any hot topic or issue related to the dysfunction in their relationship. This exercise may not involve potential conflict areas, and at times does not necessitate the use of the *Conflict Resolution Notebook.*

We suggest one person speak for three to five minutes. The other person listens, makes direct eye contact, but does not speak or interrupt. After the person who started the conversation has finished speaking, the listener responds by repeating what was just said. The speaker decides if the listener was accurate. The speaker will then clarify any miscommunication in a non-threatening, respectful manner. If miscommunication has occurred, the speaker will seek to clarify the statement(s) in question so the listener can better understand the content of the statement.

During this exercise, the couple is asked to avoid changing the subject, and to remain focused on the topic introduced by the speaker. The exercise continues until both agree on the content that was discussed.

To continue the exercise, the roles of the speaker and the listener are reversed. Now the listener becomes the speaker and introduces a topic to discuss. The previous speaker becomes the listener, and the exercise resumes as previously described. A general rule is to discuss only one topic area at a time and to keep the topic area neutral.

As previously stated, the couple is asked to begin this exercise by discussing only cold topic areas. Once the couple has improved their ability to communicate, medium, and ultimately, hot-topic areas are introduced. We prefer to help the couple decide when they are ready to discuss medium and hot topics as evidenced by their interactions in our therapy sessions. We also recommend the use of the *Conflict Resolution Notebook* for discussions of important medium and hot topics as they arise.

It is vitally important for the couple not to progress from one topic to another until *both* marital partners are comfortable with moving on. There is no predetermined speed or need to rush through this assignment. The couple must also acknowledge that they will encounter setbacks. A setback occurs when there is a need to revisit a specific topic area that remains an issue for them. We tell our couples to expect setbacks. We consider them normal and often necessary. Learning to communicate effectively is not a linear process. There are lots of twists and turns along the way. Some topics are complicated and carry much emotional baggage. It is impossible to resolve them in one, two, or three or more conversations.

If a *hot topic* must be discussed early in therapy, then the spouse with the salient issue states the need to talk while the other spouse listens. Due to the potentially explosive content being addressed, the listener may at any time respond by stating, "I need a time out; let's resume talking later in perhaps forty-five or ninety minutes." This delay is useful to diffuse the intensity of the topic being discussed, as well as the intensity of the reaction to the specific topic area. Of course, the hotter the topic, the longer the delay may take. When the couple resumes their discussion, the technique described in the communication exercise is suggested. Again, one person speaks while the other listens. Then the listener states what he or she has heard. The speaker clarifies if this is accurate, and restates the comment if necessary. This process continues until both persons agree they understand the content of the subject being discussed. It is important to restate that in hot and medium topic discussions, the use of the *Conflict Resolution Notebook* is often essential.

We have observed that couples who practice listening to each other become better at attending to both the words their spouse uses and the content or meaning behind the words. They learn to be more patient with each other by practicing not interrupting when their spouse is speaking. This exercise helps the couple to appreciate their differences and to accept each other as having something important to say. It also helps each spouse to better understand his or her partner's needs and style of communication. In our therapy sessions, we review the progress the couple is making by using recommended communication exercises. We may ask them to repeat the exercise they had at home so we may help them identify areas where they need to improve their speaking, listening, and interpreting skills.

Coping Styles in Dealing with Conflicts

We have observed different patterns in coping strategies individuals use when they are faced with discussing a *hot, medium,* or *cold* topic area with their spouses. Some individuals are *avoidant.* They may change the subject, walk away, or completely ignore their partner who is trying to discuss an issue. They become overwhelmed at feeling an uncomfortable emotion, be it fear, anger, or resentment. They attempt to avoid conflict with their spouse so they can escape from feeling these uncomfortable emotions. These individuals benefit from understanding the negative effect they have on the relationship when they are unable to discuss pertinent issues. Individual therapy is used to help the avoidant person gain insight and learn effective strategies to cope with overwhelming and frightening feelings that may have historically been provoked by discussion of conflict areas.

The *expressive* individual is able to describe thoughts and feelings easily. This person is usually in touch with his or her feelings, and is willing and able to share them. He may become impatient with a spouse who is less willing or able to express herself as easily.

The *talkative* person is different from the *expressive* person. The talkative person talks too much, and rarely allows anyone else a chance to state how she thinks or feels. He is similar to the avoidant person as he often feels anxious during important discussions. By being overly expressive, he tries to control or perhaps dominate the discussion. When this occurs, nothing is resolved. Since the *talkative* person is so difficult to talk to, important discussions are often avoided. The *talkative* person would also benefit from individual therapy sessions to discuss the cause of his anxiety and the need to control important discussions.

The *quiet* spouse neither avoids nor expresses his views. This person has a loss of words, and may not know how to respond in a given situation. The *quiet* spouse may lack skills in how to conduct a conversation, have a poor grasp of the vocabulary needed to express needs or wants adequately, or may lack assertiveness training, ample information or strong opinions about the subject being discussed. The *quiet* spouse will generally not speak up and therefore should be asked for his opinion. Gentle encouragement can be offered to help this individual feel his comments are both valued and needed.

We have observed that spouses often share both effective and ineffective communication styles. In therapy we attempt to explain how some styles may be useful and others problematic as the couple attempts to cope with difficult situations. We help our couples understand they can resolve their differences by recognizing and understanding how each spouse copes with difficult situations, and how they can work effectively with each other despite these differences. Let's meet Lila and Mark, who had a most interesting conversational style.

Lila and Mark were a married couple who was what we call, "parallel speakers." They could not let each other say a word without interrupting each other. They often spoke at the same time and, consequently, could not really hear each other. This prompted each of them to speak louder and louder until they were standing up and shouting at each other. At this point in the conversation, fingers were being pointed at one another giving the impression they were ready to come to blows. Looking at them was similar to watching the daytime talk shows where bouncers are present to prevent broken bones and bloodshed. Unfortunately, my husband and I are not trained as bouncers, and were at times worried the couple might indeed try to hurt each other and we would have to call 911! Fortunately for all concerned, the heated conversations never escalated to this extent.

We asked this couple to explain the purpose of communicating in such an ineffectual way. Lila and Mark were both surprised that we considered their communication style "ineffectual." To them it was a way for each of them to quickly make a point before they forgot what they wanted to say. They each wanted to make sure they were immediately addressing the point the other was making. They both felt there was no time to wait to state their opinion. They admitted that each of them had to have the last word. At this point we were relieved to see at least they agreed on something, even if it was to explain why they could not communicate effectively.

The problem inherent in Lila and Mark's unique style of communicating was that they could not resolve their differences, since they were too busy making their statements. They were both speakers, so no one ever functioned as the listener. The other obvious problem was that they were unable to truly *hear* each other. They heard words loudly tossed in the air, but did not give themselves time to interpret the meaning of those very important words. It was obvious their style of communication was ineffectual, indeed.

It took Lila and Mark three weeks to succeed in practicing our prescribed communication exercises. They continued to verbally get in each other's way. It was very difficult for them to take turns speaking. It was equally difficult for each of them to quietly listen to what the other was saying. But once they caught on, they had to admit they enjoyed listening to each other, and were finally able to discuss issues they had been avoiding by using parallel conversation.

Family Meetings

Once our couples have learned to *hear* and *attend* to each other in conversation, an additional communication exercise is added to their existent homework assignments.

The couple is asked to hold weekly family planning meetings, as further discussed in chapter 11. During this meeting, the couple reviews plans for the upcoming week with each other and their immediate family members. They discuss what needs to be accomplished that week, what appointments are scheduled, what chores need to be completed, and the reasons why certain tasks need to be done during that week. In the meeting, each person is assigned a desired goal. This may include doing tasks when assigned, completing tasks in a required time period, improving proficiency in a given assignment, cooperating with a mate or sibling while performing a given task, and so forth. Each family member is expected to fully commit to these assignments. A dry erase board or calendar is used to mark the scheduled appointments. A *chore list* is made to record the names of all family members, the tasks that must be performed by these individuals, and the exact date the task must be completed. In addition, a family member is assigned to be the meeting recorder. Minutes from each meeting are recorded in a *Family Meeting Notebook*. Each entry is signed and dated by all who attended the meeting. At the start of the next meeting, the meeting recorder reads the minutes from the prior meeting.

The couple (and other family members) must agree to divide up all chores and responsibilities fairly. An assessment is made regarding the ability and maturity level that is required for each task before assignments are made. The couple and immediate family members are asked to consider omitting outside appointments and obligations deemed unnecessary and that have the potential to interfere with daily scheduling of important family commitments. The family unit is therefore seen as a priority for each family member. Outside obligations may be seen as falling second compared to those required by the family unit.

As stated above, at the beginning of each family meeting, the recorder of the previous meeting needs to read the minutes from that meeting. The minutes are located in the *Family Meeting Notebook*. During the meeting, the *chore list* is also reviewed. Each family member is given a few minutes to report on the progress he or she has made regarding their assigned tasks during the preceding week. We look at patterns of progress or lack of progress in completing assigned tasks. We determine specific areas where the couple and their family need to improve as they practice working together as a unit.

Our recommended family meetings and use of calendars or dry erase boards helps the couple and their children know exactly what each other has scheduled for the day. They are aware of what they may reasonably expect from one another. We ask the couple and their children to inform each other when they will be home on a daily basis. They are to call in advance if they are going to be late, and must give a reasonable rationale why this is occurring. The family meeting format encourages partnership and an esprit de corps. If assigned chores and responsibilities are chronically not completed, or if lateness or absence is an issue, we discuss what can be causing this resistance from one or both spouses and/or their children. We must examine reasons why certain family members refuse to do their fair share of the relationship workload. We discuss what happens at home when one spouse does assigned chores and the other neglects to do so. We want to know how the couple attempts to resolve this imbalance in their relationship. We also want to know if one spouse allows one or all of their children to ignore their assigned tasks, and how this discrepancy is managed in family meetings.

At times in the early stage of therapy, one or both marital partners will test limits and fail to follow through on completing expected tasks. This often occurs when one spouse loses patience and completes tasks that belong to their spouse or to another member of the family. Once this pattern is set, the partner or family member who neglects his or her chores will continue to do so if he or she believes if they wait long enough, the chore will eventually be done by someone else. Yet this behavior is short-lived once the person sees the benefit of complying with the program. At this point we essentially take the temperature of the relationship and assess whether the couple is ready for marital therapy. As stated, we may determine they would each benefit from individual therapy sessions to work on issues that are competing with the marital therapy process. After a course of individual therapy, we resolve to bring our couple back into the marital therapy format.

WHEN COUPLES RESIST TREATMENT

Of course there are occasions when marital therapy is terminated. This occurs when we determine that one or both members of the couple are not amenable to work on the relationship. This unfortunately occurred with Peg and Tim. They were a married couple who filled every day with appointments, parties, guests, extensive travel, and constant obligations. They rarely held suggested family meetings because they "didn't have time." They didn't even have sufficient time to write appointments on a calendar. Their schedules were so busy that their relationship suffocated from the constant tension and pressure produced by not having time to breathe. As a result of hiding from one another among a constant sea of visitors and parties, they lost contact with each other as a couple. They no longer knew who Peg and Tim were. Each marital partner became "one of the crowd."

In therapy we challenged their lifestyle and suggested they have regularly scheduled meetings to determine how to drop a majority of the appointments and obligations that filled their time. They were encouraged to spend more time with each other. In conversation they were prompted to practice making eye contact, do the suggested communication exercises, and to spend time just being alone so they could enjoy quiet time together. When they agreed to spend more time together, they found they had little, if anything, to say to each other. They had essentially become strangers to one another. Ultimately they separated and left therapy.

It is not unusual for couples to avoid togetherness when faced with the ultimate conclusion that they are no longer interested in being a couple. They are daunted by the prospect of separation, divorce, how to tell their children, what their family and close friends will say, and most importantly, how to live life alone, without a partner with whom to share life's ups and downs.

In therapy, we provide our couples with many opportunities to improve their communication skills. We help them to cope with their conflicts in a meaningful and helpful manner. Each couple is given homework assignments that enable them to practice talking to each other in new and creative ways.

We encourage our couples to use *I* statements as described in chapter 3. We want our couples to get to know each other by asking open-ended questions that require an explanation or an opinion. We help our couples to ask questions such as, "How do you feel about getting together with my parents this weekend?" instead of "Do you want to get together with my parents this weekend?" We ask them to say, "Where would you like to go on vacation?" instead of making a self-centered statement such as "I want to go to Miami for our vacation, don't you?"

We help our couples to learn to both explore and express their thoughts, feelings, and opinions with confidence and respect for each other. We teach them to avoid second guessing their spouses or make assumptions that since their spouse "knows them well, he ought to know what she thinks or how she feels." We correct our couples when they say to each other, "You ought to know how I feel, we have been married long enough!" Or, "You should know by now what I want for my birthday; I shouldn't have to tell you!" We remind our couples that unless a person is truly psychic, no one, not even a mate of thirty years, has access to how we feel, what we think, or what we want unless we directly communicate this information to him. We help our couples feel less frightened when they want to convey an important thought or feeling to their significant other. We do this by teaching them how to express themselves by using language that is clear and concise.

We teach our couples to be great listeners by encouraging them to be silent when their marital partner is speaking. We then give the listener the opportunity to repeat what her spouse has said. This exercise truly strengthens a person's listening skills as well as helps her demonstrate that she is being fully attentive to her spouse.

We help our couples to communicate more effectively by encouraging them to attend to verbal and nonverbal cues used in conversation. Facial expressions, direct or indirect eye contact, tone of voice, and hand and body gestures are all important pieces of information to consider when a couple is attempting to communicate.

Facial expressions indicate emotion, sometimes far better and more directly than words. A person may use kind words, but communicate conflicting feelings by having an angry facial expression. In therapy, we help couples be aware of giving mixed or conflicting information. We encourage them to use words and facial expressions that are consistent so their mates can fully understand not only the words that are said but also the meaning behind the words being conveyed.

We emphasize the use of direct eye contact. It is most disconcerting when one spouse is speaking and her mate is looking elsewhere. We help our couples to look directly at each other when they are communicating. When we observe indirect eye contact, we discuss the reasons this may be occurring, and help the couple understand that direct eye contact and effective communication go hand and hand.

We have noted the tone of voice one uses to communicate is usually easy for our couples to understand. It is hard to ignore and misinterpret an angry, sad, or happy tone of voice. At times our couples use an angry or argumentative tone of voice not only to express their anger, but also to intimidate or manipulate their spouse into submitting to their wishes. When a person's tone of voice seems exaggerated or out of context with the words being used or the situation at hand, we provide feedback on how to modulate one's tone of voice. We teach the speaker to use a tone of voice that is consistent with the words he or she expresses. We also help couples become more aware of their motives when expressing anger. We help them to understand that controlling and manipulative behavior only serves to create resentment and can weaken a relationship already in jeopardy.

We also examine the affect or emotions being expressed by the couple. This may include anger, fear, frustration, or joy. We discourage the use of emotional blackmail such as destructive efforts to put a spouse down, insisting that a spouse is always or often wrong, or putting all the blame for a given problem on a spouse's shoulders. Conversely, we help our couples to discuss their issues with openness rather than defensiveness. We help them to use teamwork to arrive at workable resolutions to their problems.

Body Language

Body language and hand gestures are often used in communication. In some cultures hand gestures are used more than others, especially in the European countries. Arms folded across the chest, shaking a fist, or pointing an index finger may be signs of an angry or frustrated individual. A downcast head, averted eyes, or arms hanging down the sides of the body could indicate embarrassment, shyness, or sadness. We help our couples to both translate each other's body language, and use gestures that are considerate and appropriate. For example, shaking a fist at a spouse is not an appropriate gesture,

nor is pointing a finger in a spouse's face. We review the use of both appropriate and inappropriate physical gestures as we help our couples communicate more effectively.

Part of body language is eye contact. We encourage our couples to make
direct eye contact with each other when they are conversing. Naturally we
are not intending one spouse stare down the other, but rather to attend to the
person who is conversing with you. In our culture it is considered rude to
essentially look away from someone who is addressing you. When a person
looks away during a conversation, it appears the person feels guilty, is terribly shy, or is trying to avoid conversing about what is being said.

Again, we discourage the use of intimidating tactics or evasive gestures
both in and between our sessions. Our goal is to help our couples support
each other and see each other as equals in a potentially healthy relationship.

Marital or relationship therapy is the time for couples to learn to listen
attentively to one another. They are asked to support each other's efforts to
improve their relationship, remain positive, be genuine and loving despite
their individual differences and struggles so they can find the common good
that binds them as a couple.

Chapter Five

The Mystique of Compatibility

In the preceding chapters, we discussed how our couples can improve their understanding and communication skills. We consider these skills essential for couples who are determined to stay together and enjoy the ability to speak and be heard by their spouses. When daily issues related to cold, medium and hot topics emerge, our couples will feel less overwhelmed when they have learned techniques to effectively handle a variety of stressful issues.

We are aware that knowing how to implement these important techniques is only part of what contributes to a happy relationship. Whether a couple is dating, engaged, or married, *compatibility* is the essential glue that binds a couple's commitment and devotion to one another year after year. The couples who we have interviewed agreed compatibility is the cornerstone of a forever relationship, but few of them can define what *compatibility* means to them. It seems to us that *compatibility is that ambiguous sense of fitting together*. Further stated, it is a couple who stays together in harmony. It is the stable couple who is able to integrate their ideas and lifestyle without an abundance of strife and rejection. It is the couple who respects each other, and remains congenial despite the ups and downs of everyday existence. It is that "je ne sais quoi" that contributes to the couple's sense of belonging together. Granted no relationship is perfect, or without arguments and issues, but the compatible couple is better able to cope with these dips in their relationship without fragmentation and prolonged periods of anger and un-happiness. As we ponder this concept, we question whether compatibility is tangible or intangible. Can we teach our couples to be compatible by providing the skills to help them fit together?

I dare say compatibility is not something that can be purchased or easily acquired. Yet we can see it in couples who seem to just fit together despite the dips in their relationships that have caused them to initiate therapy. What happens when these very same couples break up? Have they lost their compatibility, or were we wrong to assume they possessed that *je ne sais quoi* from the start? Indeed, I have met couples along the way, in and out of the therapy milieu, who seemed to "have it all." In most cases I was certainly surprised to later find out I was wrong. They simply did not have compatibility. They simply did not belong together. One such couple, Wendy and John, I met in graduate school. I was single at the time and would occasionally spend time with them. They were a very attractive couple. I thought they were the couple to aspire to, the best of the best. After we finished school, I temporarily lost touch with Wendy and John until I received a note from Wendy a few years later. She informed me she and John were getting a divorce. I immediately called Wendy and invited her over for dinner. While we enjoyed our meal, she related why she and John split up. I was shocked as she recounted the way John emotionally abused and physically threatened her throughout their relationship; even during the time I thought they were the "perfect couple."

So you see we can all be tricked by couples who appear to be happy, only to find out compatibility eluded them as well. It is my perception that some couples actually put on an act when in public. They try to project the image of a blissfully happy couple. We have all seen couples who are overly affectionate or repeatedly call each other *honey* or *sweetheart, or say* "I love you" again and again in public. For example, I was having lunch with a co-worker who called her husband after we finished our meal. At the conclusion of their short telephone call, she repeated "I love you" several times before ending the call. I could not help but feel concerned about their relationship. I wondered who she was trying to convince of her love, her husband or herself.

Compatibility and Attraction

In this chapter, we analyze what we believe are the components of compatibility. We begin with the concept of attraction, which is exemplified by the couple who is charmed or drawn together as if by magnetic force. I don't think I have ever met a compatible couple who did not find each other attractive in one way or another. It is of course possible for a couple to not be initially attracted to one another. In fact, many of our couples have said when they first met they didn't think their partner was their *type*. When we pry deeper into what their *type* is, the reply is always something quite tangible. It seems each person develops an idea of what the perfect mate should look like, how he or she should behave both in private and in public, what they do for a living, where they live, what type of car they drive, and so forth. This is an individual stereotype to which all potential dates and eventually mates are compared. The ideal date or mate may be blond, tall, short, or dark haired.

They may have a moustache or be clean-shaven. They may be athletic or intellectual. They may have a dimple or a crooked smile. As we all know, physical attractiveness is indeed in the eyes of the beholder.

We have learned from our couples that when they began dating, they pursued their ideal companion from their individual stereotype. Yet as they gained more experience in the dating arena, many of these same individuals began looking for different traits in a companion. Yet others did date men and women who fit their stereotype only to find out the traits they originally wanted in a partner weren't enough to satisfy them. There are countless persons who have stated about their mates "they were good looking until I got to know them better, then they weren't so good looking any more." Indeed we have heard many describe their current mates as persons who they did not find attractive initially, but who "grew on them" as they got to know them. So a good sense of humor, a keen wit, or the way one cocks his head when he smiles may be the traits that one looks for after learning that dimples and steel blue eyes are only skin deep.

Socioeconomic Status

Many of us remember such films as *To Marry a Millionaire*. The premise was to find a rich man to marry and live happily-ever-after. Of course, *gold diggers* are alive and well, even in this day and age. Some women and men believe if they were rich they would be happy. I have heard patients who are still looking for Mr. or Ms. Right say they "don't care what the person they marry looks like, as long as he or she is rich and can support them in fine fashion." The question remains: are the rich attracted to the poor as much as the poor are attracted to the rich? How many princes and princesses look for paupers to live with in wedded bliss? How many successful movie stars look for their future mates in the local supermarket on *singles mingle* nights? My point is that in our experience we have found people often gravitate to those of a similar socioeconomic status, or at least to those who have a similar attitude toward money and how it should be earned and spent. So it isn't that the rich only marry the rich, and the poor only marry the poor. It is the way the couple earns, spends, and saves money that may determine a couple's level of compatibility. Persons in search of a compatible partner must also consider if their potential mate is generous with money. A person may be wealthy and stingy at the same time! We will now meet Megan and Jim, who had different attitudes about money. Megan was a hardworking teacher who made a decent salary. She met Jim, who made his living at the track betting on horses. He was rich one day and poor the next. Megan liked Jim, but could not imagine marrying him since she did not respect his choice of career or his casual attitude toward money. The relationship ended when Jim started to ask Megan for money only to find it was gone within a week. Megan explained, "As a hard working teacher, I want someone who shares my work ethic."

I recall newlyweds Sam and Bonnie. Bonnie was a secretary and made far less money than Sam, who was an accountant. In less than six months, Bonnie ran up all of Sam's credit cards to the maximum. Bonnie's explanation was "I'm rich now so I can spend all I want." Sam was shocked at the bills he received and at "Bonnie's irresponsible attitude toward his hard earned income." He and Bonnie fought over money straight through their divorce settlement.

So I think we would all agree that an important area of compatibility is a couple's attitude toward money. After all, just ask Megan and Jim, or Bonnie and Sam!

Spirituality or Religion

There are many couples who could not imagine dating or marrying someone outside of their religion. They want a partner who shares the same ideas and beliefs in which they were raised. They want to be able to attend the same house of worship, celebrate the same holidays, and bring up their children to share their mutual religious beliefs. A general belief is that marrying a person who shares one's religion or spiritual beliefs is *simply easier* for all the reasons mentioned above. In fact, many persons seek a partner who is of the same national origin for many of the same reasons cited above.

Naturally there are many who become attracted to others who do not share their religion or national origin, but remain together because they share common goals, ethics, and core beliefs. Perhaps neither of them was brought up to be very religious. They may prefer to develop their own traditions and spiritual practices for themselves and their children. In these cases, religious or national differences proved to be the glue that makes their relationships work effectively.

Indeed, there are those who share the same religion, but were brought up to express these beliefs differently. Some persons are bought up to be more observant and strict than others when it comes to following religious doctrine. Despite the fact that they share the same religion, they may not agree on how to express these beliefs, how or where to worship, how to celebrate religious holidays, and what customs to follow when bringing up their children. In some cases, these differences can cause more dissention and prejudice than in couples who worship different religions.

So it seems part of compatibility involves sharing similar spiritual beliefs and customs. Or perhaps agreeing to create new traditions based on a couple's views of a Supreme Being, the afterlife, as well as how to celebrate holidays, following certain customs, and rearing of children. Compatibility always involves the ability and willingness to be respectful and understanding of the differences that exist in a given relationship.

Personal Habits

Let's reflect on the movie and subsequent television show *The Odd Couple*. Oscar and Felix were both opposites regarding their personal habits. Despite their differences, they were best friends. Oscar was a *slob* and Felix a *neat freak*. Even though they had very different personal habits, and occasional bickering and complaining about their differences, they were able to remain roommates. In their own way, they were compatible as roommates.

We tend to take our personal habits for granted until someone close to us remarks they are unusual or unacceptable. Some folks are pack rats, while others love to throw away what they perceive as unwanted items. Some people shower daily, while others bathe less often. Some individuals need lots of alone time and physical space to breathe unencumbered. Their counterparts may prefer the comfort and closeness of togetherness or of a lifestyle in which other friends or family members are often present.

We tend to view disparate personal habits as cute or perhaps charming in the first weeks or months of a relationship. Yet these insidious behaviors can be real deal breakers in a more serious relationship. Most people do not want to tolerate a messy bathroom, or socks thrown on the dining room table when living with the messy individual, no matter how much they love him or her.

Social Habits

Other personal habits to consider are whether a potential mate is a loner or a party person. Some of our couples have had arguments over these differences. We met Carol who prefers to stay at home after work, relax, watch television, or read a book. Her husband Matt enjoys his free time at the local restaurant/bar where his friends meet in the evenings to unwind and socialize. Carol complained that Matt prefers the company of his friends to staying at home with her. She worried that he found her boring or uninteresting as a mate. Matt was not bored with his wife, and repeatedly asked her to join him in his outings. This couple was asked to compromise regarding how they spent their free time. Carol was encouraged to join Matt with his friends once or twice a week. Matt was encouraged to stay home with Carol after work one or two nights a week. Both were encouraged to have date nights at least once a week in which friends were not included. This arrangement seemed to suite them just fine.

Song Bird or Night Owl Issues

We have observed compatibility issues between morning song birds and night owls. One person traditionally wakes up early. He or she likes to rise early and get going on their day. They may start their day with chores, exercise, or running errands. Due to being an early riser, the song bird may prefer to be early to bed as well. Conversely, the night owl loves to sleep in, especially on weekends and on vacation when there is no need to get up early for work. The night owl does not want to be awakened by the song bird, and may get testy when this occurs. The night owl also prefers a later night life, of which the song bird may not be a fan. Issues arise when the song bird wants the night owl to join in on the morning run or the early trip to the supermarket, or when the night owl wants the song bird to stay up and watch the sunrise together. Again, sacrifice and willingness to compromise is the key to success in these relationships. Sometimes the night owl needs to get up early to bird watch with the song bird. The song bird needs to occasionally stay up to watch the ball drop on New Year's Eve.

Personal Habits

There are other personal habits that can create compatibility issues when not appropriately addressed. For example, one mate may prefer to eat three meals a day at the exact same time, while her partner prefers to graze when the mood strikes. We all know those who desperately need a cup of strong coffee in the morning or a cigarette to start the day, versus those who easily pop out of bed and energetically start their day without benefit of caffeine or nicotine.

These personal habits are all important aspects of the individuality we exhibit on a daily basis. They neither make us good or bad, right or wrong, merely different from one another. Compatible couples need not share the same personal habits to be happy, but they must accept each other's differences and be willing to amend those habits that are truly offensive to their mate, let alone to the general population. Remember the example of socks thrown on the dining room table? That's a personal habit that most of us would find offensive. We suggest that each individual compromise, negotiate, and gain insight into their personal habits that may negatively affect others. The willingness to compromise and negotiate is vitally important for compatibility to exist in a special relationship.

Racial Issues

During the last few decades, our society has made efforts toward advancing the equality of persons of different races. Yet individual families may not have caught up with the rest of society. It is one thing to be accepted and loved by an individual of a different race or culture, but this acceptance may be lacking among key family members whose prejudice or negative attitudes can deeply wound a delicate romantic relationship.

A future husband's parents or grandparents may not be willing to share their lives with a young woman of a different race or cultural background. They may make negative comments about how society will treat the young couple and their future children if the couple decides to wed. More accurately, they may be commenting about how they will feel if the couple marries. Certain families are closed off from or perhaps uncomfortable with those persons different from themselves. They may react in a clannish manner and use rejection to scare away the unwanted person who is looking for acceptance in their family. The family members may simply state their belief that persons of different races are not compatible with one another due to their cultural differences. We believe it is the couple's responsibility to explore their deepest beliefs to determine if they regard themselves as truly compatible and thereby accepting of the differences that exist between them. If the couple is determined to stay together, they must be equally determined to confront their families. They may tell their families that they respect their feelings, but the fate of their relationship will not be determined by the opinions of others, no matter how much they love and respect them.

Education and Intelligence

One of the best places to look for a potential mate is in the halls of higher learning. A simple gander from one's seat in a lecture hall offers a panoramic view of potential suitors. Choices abound of men and women who may share the same career aspirations and attitudes, intellectual curiosity, love for learning, and interest in personal growth. Those who have found their studious soul mate may share these important values and possess the essential foundation of a compatible romantic relationship or friendship.

We are not suggesting we believe a measure of compatibility is found by reviewing a couple's curriculum vitae or scholastic achievements. Yet we have found a similarity in intellectual curiosity, sharp wit or style of humor, knowledge of similar vocabulary, interest in some of the same subject areas, as well as in local and world affairs, and cultural pursuits gives a couple advantages over those who do not share these interests. Let's meet Diane and Joe, who did not share the same educational background.

Diane and Joe were an interesting couple and a study of contrasts. Diane was from rural Tennessee. She earned her high school diploma admittedly "by the skin of her teeth." Joe was from Los Angeles and earned a PhD in physics from UCLA. They met when Joe traveled to Tennessee to attend a friend's wedding. Diane sat at his table at the reception and looked charming in her puffy bridesmaid dress. Her southern accent and outgoing personality were attractive to Joe who was rather intellectual, quiet, and shy. Diane found Joe to be a challenge since he was so different from the men she met in her home town. She enjoyed teaching him a few dance steps during the reception and Joe enjoyed the attention. They were married four months later.

Within the first year of marriage the signs of strain in their incompatible relationship began to show. Joe grew ashamed of Diane, especially when they were with his highly educated friends from work. He rolled his eyes whenever Diane used incorrect grammar and made statements such as "I might could do that." Diane hated his criticism and found him rigid and controlling. The last straw was when Joe bought Diane an English grammar textbook for Christmas.

In therapy Diane complained that Joe was just "not her type." She wanted someone who was more fun and less uptight. Joe wanted a woman of whom he could be proud and with whom he could share his intellectual interests and skills. The lack of compatibility between Diane and Joe proved to be as stated above, "the last straw."

Communication Skills

In the previous chapters, we discussed techniques we teach to our couples to improve their communication skills. An area of compatibility pertains to how each partner expresses himself when he is angry or sad, happy or frightened. In the previous section, we discussed Diane and Joe. They were incompatible due to their differences in educational achievement as well as in their style of communication, especially in the way they expressed their feelings. Diane was very outspoken. When she was angry, everyone knew. Joe, on the other hand, kept his thoughts and feelings more contained. He was very reserved and found expressions of anger to be "boorish." As stated, he would roll his eyes to show his discontent with Diane, but would not verbalize his feelings to her except when he used concepts and vocabulary Diane did not understand. Consequently, their style of communication was incompatible as well. They divorced after five years of marriage.

Sexuality and Affection

The sexual liberation of the 1960s and 1970s greatly changed the way sexuality and public affection are currently viewed and expressed. The idea that one must be married to be sexually active has vastly changed in the American culture. Yet we have found that the fear of contacting HIV, AIDS, and other sexually transmitted diseases, as well as the threat of unwanted pregnancy seems to be turning the pendulum ever so slightly in a more conservative direction. There have been couples in our practice who demonstrated more restraint regarding *free love* than in previous years. More single couples emphasize the need for *safe sex* and ultimately abstain from sexual relations before marriage or consciously use birth control methods to feel more assured they are preventing unwanted pregnancy and remaining disease free.

Anna and Jeff were a study in contrast in terms of their attitudes toward intimacy and pregnancy. Anna and Jeff were engaged at the time we saw them in therapy. Anna didn't seem to care if she got pregnant, since she knew she wanted to marry Jeff, and she definitely wanted to have children with him—the sooner the better! Jeff on the other hand did not want to be a father quite yet, or be expecting a child before they got married. He did not want his bride to walk down the aisle in a maternity wedding dress.

Anna told Jeff she was "on the pill" and she preferred that he *not* use a condom because she found it "unnatural." Jeff feared Anna was not taking her pills regularly and felt wearing a condom was necessary to prevent an unwanted pregnancy. Their disagreement over the use of birth control caused Anna and Jeff to have sexual relations much less frequently. This almost resulted in postponing their wedding.

Jessie and John also disagreed about sexual attitudes and mores. Jessie and John were "going steady" when they started therapy. John had been sexually active before he met Jessie. On the other hand, Jessie was a virgin and only "made out" with a few guys before dating John. Jessie wanted to move slowly and was barely tolerant of John "petting" her even while she was wearing clothing. John was very attracted to Jessie and wanted to "go all the way." He purchased a book that diagramed *one hundred sexual positions* he hoped to try with Jessie. During the course of therapy, Jessie got the courage to admit that her religious and moral beliefs dictated she be a virgin bride. She was willing to "make out" and even "pet," but could not go further despite her love and sexual attraction to John. It was clear that Jessie and John were in two very separate places in their desire for intimacy and sexuality. In therapy we encouraged them to accept and respect each other's needs, thoughts, and desires about intimacy in order to stay together as a couple. We explained one should not use force, guilt, emotional blackmail, or any other manipulative tactics to persuade a partner to have sexual relations before he or she is ready. John agreed to accept Jessie's wishes, and admitted he respected her willingness to be her own person, and stand up for the principles and virtues she had always believed. Jessie was indeed a virgin bride. She gave birth to a baby girl a year later.

It is important to note that an aspect of compatibility among happy couples is related to how a couple expresses affection, engages in love making, as well as the frequency of intimacy. All of these areas merit discussion to determine what is comfortable for each individual. One marital partner will inevitably be more affectionate or desirous of more frequent love making than the other. In the same vein, one person may be more adventurous in regards to the type of sexual positions he or she prefers, as well as the use of sexual aids or toys. There will likely be a difference in the level of prior sexual experience and the number of previous sexual partners they both had. Patience and acceptance are very important in order to allow a loved one sufficient time to consider if they are comfortable expressing more adventurous lovemaking methods. Of course differences in sexual preference, be it homosexuality or heterosexuality, must be known in advance of marriage or a serious relationship. It is only fair to reveal a preference for a partner of the same sex if leaning toward dating or becoming serious with someone of the opposite sex.

We have found it is important and yet difficult for couples to put their shyness aside and discuss their sexual beliefs, needs, and habits prior to entering into a committed relationship. Yet we encourage our couples to discuss their sexual needs and desires so they can openly address differences of attitudes and preferences that may pose a stumbling block in their relationship.

Indeed, as couples face life's complicated stressors, deal with advancing age, illness, symptoms of change of life, and shifts in body shape and fitness levels, habits of sexual intimacy may be temporarily affected. Communication and compatibility are the keys to surviving the bumps and turns of sexual and romantic expression.

Whenever we meet with a couple, we encourage them to openly and truthfully examine the various aspects of compatibility that we reviewed in this chapter. We urge our dating and engaged couples to share their attitudes and ideas toward sexuality, religion, aspects of their personal habits, and so forth. We support their efforts to learn about their differences, and to begin to compromise and accommodate each other's needs early in their relationships. We teach them the importance of respecting their individual differences, and not trying to make their partner a carbon copy of themselves. By providing a "reality check," we urge them to reduce or stop doing behaviors that most other people in our society would find offensive. We also encourage them not to punish each other by doing those behaviors that especially annoy their partner. Instead, we review the use of our *conflict resolution exercises* to explore any feelings of hostility or resentment that may result in exhibiting behavior that is especially offensive to others.

It is apparent that some couples will never find a middle ground in certain aspects of their relationship. The night owl may remain the night owl. The loner may always seek special time alone to curl up with a good book and think about life. Whatever the differences may be, it is important for spouses to accept and respect those unique beliefs and behaviors that represent one's personal identity and preference, of course providing they are not beliefs and behaviors that are essential for the relationship to endure.

An essential part of compatibility for the happy couple is acceptance of a partner's lifestyle, their integrity, sense of ethics, as well as those areas of compatibility that the couple has in common. It is their goals for the future, their commitment to each other, and their enduring love and respect for their spouse's right to be a strong, independent individual, as well as one half of a super terrific couple, that will help them pass the test of time together.

Chapter Six

What Happy Couples Can Teach Us

We have had many couples in our practice who have the framework of a solid marriage. They participate in marital or relationship therapy to further improve their communication skills or to resolve minor issues before they become unmanageable. After completing our therapy program, many return for monthly maintenance therapy to further strengthen their relationships.

We have learned much from these happy couples. We have observed first hand what makes a relationship work. In this chapter we review the skills that successful and happy couples have in common.

Happy Couples, Happy Dating

Happy married couples are those who have worked hard to achieve success when they were first dating. They established and were generally faithful to a number of healthy boundaries and guidelines they created together. Many decided they were a couple and functioned as such, rather than as of two distinct individuals. Together they defined what being a couple means to them. For example, being a couple often means they are focused on and loyal to one another. Each person made the other a priority. Each person was fully committed to the other. There was an effort to regularly spend quality time together in order to create fond memories to hold dear forever.

The happy dating couples we met in therapy were honest from the beginning of their relationships on how they felt about issues such as differences in religion, political affiliation, and whether they wanted to have children. They shared their attitudes and opinions on where they would like to live, if they wanted to pursue higher education, whether they wanted to own pets, if they were night owls or were individuals who were early to bed and early to rise. In other words, they honestly and openly discussed all the issues that constitute compatibility as discussed in chapter 5.

When these happy couples became engaged and later married, they knew each other very well and had already discussed and resolved major topic areas that have the potential to destroy a relationship that is less solid. We encourage dating and engaged couples to come into relationship therapy early in their relationships. We provide helpful tips on how to discuss their issues, resolve conflicts, and develop the framework for a successful marital relationship.

Genuine Versus Pseudo-Closeness

We observe our happy couples achieve genuine closeness rather than pseudo-closeness in their relationships. By doing so, they decrease distance that can result in secrets, separate lives, and ultimately separation and/or divorce. Genuine closeness occurs when a couple takes their time to know each other. They have spent much time doing lots of different activities together, and have observed each other in many different situations with a variety of different people. Over time they develop a closeness that is originally defined as friendship and later as best friends who are also in love. They are not in a hurry to get engaged or married. Rather they nurture their time together and carefully assess if they are truly compatible. In so doing, they identify and address the apparent *red flags* that may exist. If they observe behavior that is disquieting or presents a potential problem, they discuss it together rather than keep it to themselves attempting to find excuses for it. Therefore, they trust each other enough to take risks in discussing important matters before they get worse.

Pseudo-closeness occurs when a couple is very eager to become a couple. They may choose to do this to avoid loneliness, in response to family or peer pressure to be involved with someone, or their biological clock is loudly ticking. Other couples are quick to achieve pseudo-closeness because of their desire to leave an unhappy life with parents or another failing relationship. Some are in search of monetary support so they can pay off debts or not need to work at all. Others find comfort in quickly establishing a relationship when they find they are pregnant, or are suddenly a single parent. Others feel entering into a relationship affords them status with family and friends who regard single individuals as somehow inferior or lacking skills to find a mate. Pseudo-close couples quickly present themselves as a couple to their friends and co-workers. They attend family functions as an established couple. In their eagerness, they may even live together or get married before they have taken the time to ascertain if they are truly compatible or have established a meaningful bond that happy couples share.

I remember a summer psychology class I took in college. It has been many years since I took this class, but a couple I met there made a lasting impression on me. From day one, this man and woman sat closely together in class. Their eyes locked as they held hands and hugged before (sometimes during) and after class. They appeared inseparable. By the way they acted I thought they had been going together for a long time. Toward the middle of the semester, I remember learning they had just met during registration for the class we had together. That means they had only known each other for a few weeks! I don't know what happened to their relationship after the class ended, but it certainly appeared they were in a big hurry to present themselves as if they were an established couple to get attention from everyone in the classroom. They succeeded in doing the latter, but ultimately did not convince their classmates they indeed were a couple who had the makings of a love that would stand the test of time.

I Versus We, Me Versus Us

It stands to reason that happy couples get together for the right reasons and do not announce they are a couple until their closeness is genuine. In terms of genuine closeness and ones identification as a "couple," we must ask ourselves, "When does one become a couple?" When does *I become we,* or *me become us*? When does *mine* become *ours*? Let's see if we can learn the answers to these questions from Carmen and Jose.

Carmen and Jose were recently engaged. They took their first vacation together and couldn't wait to tell everyone what fun they had. Carmen told her best girlfriends, "I went snorkeling, I did lots of shopping, I ate in four star restaurants." Jose told his friends, "We went to the beach, we took carriage rides, we bought souvenirs for everyone," and so forth. Jose was very hurt that Carmen used the word *I* instead of *we* or *us*. In a therapy session, Carmen explained they are not going to be *we* or *us* until or unless they get married. Her explanation saddened Jose. It made him feel somewhat distant from Carmen. According to Jose, they were already a close couple who deserved to be referred to as *we* and *us*.

As we discussed their relationship, we learned Carmen indeed wanted the distance her behavior implied. She enjoyed her adventures with Jose, but didn't really think she and Jose were a *genuine* couple because they were not married. Until her wedding day, she thought they were "hanging out together," despite the diamond ring on her finger. A disconcerted Jose suggested they "hang out together" a while longer before deciding when or even if they should get married. Good for Jose! He had the good sense to recognize it is important to become a genuine couple well in advance of the marriage ceremony. He understood the bond that happy couples make when they identify themselves to each other and the world as a solid unit. Indeed, there are many marital couples who, despite spending several years together, have not learned what happy couples know: commitment means that *I* becomes *we*, that *me* becomes *us*.

Let's meet Todd and Julia who were married for twenty years, but Todd continued to ask Julia if he could borrow *her* camera (the one he got her for her birthday) to photograph their prize rose tree. He asked if he could use *her* scissors to cut an ad out of the paper, and if they would use *her* car for the weekend since his car was making a suspicious noise. Julia controlled what they watched on *her* television, and decided whether or not Todd could use *her* computer to check *their* e-mail.

This couple had not learned that happy couples don't often distinguish between *mine* and *yours* when it comes to household items they *both* use and share. In contrast, happy couples would generally refer to *the* camera, or "the one I got you," *the* scissors, *our* car, *our* television, and *our* computer.

So that brings us back to "when does *I* become *we* or *me* become *us*?" It seems this transition occurs when a couple truly sees themselves as a unit. It is apparent they have agreed to face the world together rather than apart. They can appreciate the contributions each makes to the relationship, and do not feel the need to control each other by using their possessions as leverage. Rather, they have learned to share their lives and their possessions so they can both partake and enjoy.

Couples Who Play Well, Stay Well

When I think about couples who are happy and have a fun and fulfilling relationship versus those who don't, I am reminded of the way children learn to play together. Most children are given various opportunities to learn appropriate social skills. These opportunities arise as they interact with their parents, siblings, extended family members, neighbors, and schoolmates. Young children are very self-centered and egocentric. What they touch is theirs, what they want is theirs, and what someone else has is theirs too. As they mature, many children learn to *share* and *give* to others. They learn the pleasure and benefit from being part of a happy family, a close friendship, a social group, and very importantly, part of a society that discourages selfishness and greed.

As children mature into adolescence and adulthood, they practice these social skills be they with friends, family, neighbors, or in romantic or professional relationships. Some individuals become quite proficient at being other-centered versus egocentric. They become considerate, caring, and often willing to put others before themselves. The old saying "no, you go first" is offered in line at the bank, at a dinner party, or when a spouse cuts the cake at his wedding. And yet, it has become apparent that this sense of other-centeredness or altruism is waning in our culture. You just have to drive on our highways and watch aggressive drivers exhibit a childlike *me-first* mentality to know that a *me generation* is alive and well, and is wreaking havoc on many marriages and romantic relationships.

Unfortunately this childlike and sometimes truly narcissistic need to be *me-first* is not limited to children. Many individuals never mature beyond a *me-first* mentality. They continue to lack social awareness, integrity, and a willingness to share and cooperate with others including their mate. They lack what we call *relationship maturity.*

Relationship Maturity

Happy couples share relationship maturity. This stands for a strong sense of compassion for a partner, a striving for a solid connection that fosters integrity, ethical behavior, respect for another's feelings, and commitment to the quality and longevity of their relationship. It places the relationship above everything and everyone else. Each spouse commits to keep this sacred relationship and protects it against intruders and other harmful influences. This is a relationship that maintains "to thine own self and to each other, be true."

Best Friends

We ask our couples to think back to those relationships in their lives in which relationship maturity was present. Many of our couples state this is characteristic of the relationship they historically had and may continue to enjoy with their best friends. Most people regard a *best friend* as a special relationship. A best friend, a true friend is hard to come by. We have early memories of our best buddies, and if we are lucky, one or all of our best buddies remain in our lives today.

One hallmark of a relationship with a best friend is compatibility. Best friends have a lot in common. This may pertain to interests, backgrounds, opinions, and a common view of the world. Best friends truly enjoy each other's company and have fun when they are together. They may laugh and cry at the same movies, share intimate secrets, and keep confidences. Best friends are there for each other through thick and thin, good times and bad. Best friends fight to protect one another's dignity and honor against all odds. When one falls, the other is close by to be the rescuer. Best friends share events together, both happy and sad. They are there at your wedding; they are one of the first to hold your new baby; they dry your tears when you fear your mate is cheating; and they sit by your bedside when you are sick in the hospital.

Best friends are caring and respectful of your feelings. They don't feel the need to fight with you to feel important or in control of the relationship. When a fight or misunderstanding occurs, they are genuinely sorry and want to quickly mend this rift so the relationship can resume. Best friends don't try to take away your dignity and honor so they can feel more important or better about themselves. Best friends don't take each other for granted. Best friends are happy for your good luck and your accomplishments. They accept your differences and often agree to disagree. They accept your faults as well as your virtues.

Best friends are accepting of us and love us for who are. They know we sometimes fail, or do not do our best. They may point out our flaws, but do so in a constructive manner. They don't try to change us or turn us into their own image or who they think we should be. They don't laugh at us, but with us. They avoid negativity or gossip that would tarnish our reputation or ruin our image. They are there to support rather than destroy the essence of our being.

Best friends are patient with those who are important to them. These friends allow their loved ones to take their time to come up with solutions to their problems. They understand every one moves at their own pace and these friends are okay with that. Best friends do not rush the elaborate explanation of a story, even though their style of communication is to cut to the chase. They are able to wait for their friend to try on twenty dresses before picking the best one. They know if the tables were reversed, their best friend would patiently wait for them as well.

So why don't those who are dating, engaged, or married behave more like best friends? We believe they indeed should do so. Our happy couples tell us they are best friends with each other. They avoid using sarcasm, guilt, blame, or passive-aggressive behaviors when they interact with one another. They know that to behave in this manner causes their spouse and best friend to feel defensive, argumentative, or consequently to back off and become avoidant. They know from experience that best friends don't treat each other this way.

Best friendships, as well as happy couples, do not survive in relationships in which there is a significant amount of tension and the need to avoid each other to keep from feeling upset, nervous, and angry. They know if these circumstances were present in a best friendship, they would rarely get together, and the friendship would likely end. The same consequences occur in best friendships and in couples that exhaust each other with negativity, blame, feelings of guilt, constant complaints, and raised voices. In contrast, happy couples don't put each other through this constant drama. They support each other with positive words and deeds. They look for the good in their partner. When they disagree or are unhappy with their partner's behavior, they provide feedback by using thoughtful and constructive terminology. They make suggestions rather than give orders on what should be done. When they face conflicts, they address them quickly so they do not fester and therefore worsen over time. When a mistake has been made, there is a quick and sincere apology. As with best friends, apologies are accepted. The mistake is never brought up again, even in the heat of anger or disappointment. What is past is past. Happy couples look to the present and the future for hope and happiness. They do not dwell on the past when hard feelings or mistakes may have taken place. If the happy couple is in therapy with us, they successfully use our conflict resolution techniques.

Happy couples know each other very well. They recognize even the slightest shifts in mood, body language, and facial expressions. They are quick to address changes in these areas because they are genuinely concerned about what their spouse is thinking or feeling. They want to know if they can possibly help their spouse. The happy couple knows each other's likes and dislikes. This is done by both astute observation and questions of each other regarding preferences. Consequently, the happy couple is more likely to be correct in picking out gifts for one another. By being intimately knowledge-able about each other, and respectful of each other, they are better able to predict when a conflict or disagreement will occur. This knowledge helps the happy couple avoid the pitfalls unhappy couples experience. When conflicts occur, the happy couple can decide to either drop the issue if it's not impor-tant enough to quarrel about, or face it using positive conflict resolution techniques that we describe in this book. In addition, they are better able to address the issue before it gets to the point that it is unlikely it can be easily or successfully resolved.

Happy couples are loyal to each other. They do not gossip or say hurtful things about each other to friends or family. They always present a united front in public. They wait until they are alone with each other to express disagreements or dissatisfaction with one another.

There was once a television show called *The Newlywed Game*. Couples who were married under a year were invited to compete for prizes by answer-ing questions about their spouse. This was a very entertaining and funny show. You were able to see major differences between couples who truly knew each other as friends, and those who were essentially clueless about their mate's tastes and habits, likes and dislikes. The couples with the best answers and highest scores seemed relaxed and happy. Conversely, the cou-ples who consistently provided wrong answers would get agitated, disap-pointed, and surprised their mates didn't know the correct answers, or simply stated, didn't know them very well. This show consistently showed the im-portance of being friends with your spouse before and during marriage. Of course, being best friends is even better!

So we know friendship in committed relationships is important, but it is not entirely sufficient. Happy couples also have a unique spark that prompts them to be together as romantic couples. They enjoy being close, they want to touch each other and to explore intimate and sexual relations. This roman-tic drive is often what prompts dating couples to get engaged and later married. Our happy couples tell us they enjoy both their friendship and the sparks that continue to ignite between them, even after many years of married life together. They tell us there are normal fluctuations in the expression of these sparks. These fluctuations are present in all relationships and can be caused by life stressors, illness, fatigue, long work hours, mounting life responsibilities, depression, and so forth. Yet despite the ups and downs of married life, their best friendship keeps their relationships alive and well.

Happy couples have told us their lives are full of active as well as quiet moments. They adopt compatible hobbies and interests they enjoy sharing with one another. Or they may spend their time in parallel play. For example, one partner may be surfing the internet, while the other is reading a book. They enjoy the quiet moments when they laugh at the same commercials on television, or quietly watch it snow from the vantage point of a picture window. They may turn their noses up at the same badly prepared dish in a restaurant. They will agree the sales person in a store had a bad attitude and will exchange similar feelings about snooty people in general. Happy couples roll their eyes at the same annoying behaviors they observe or will sometimes avoid each other's glances to keep from laughing out loud in a situation that calls for a quiet or silent response.

We have noticed that happy couples give each other credit for good ideas, good taste in clothes or home furnishings, or events in their lives that work out well. For example, my husband frequently gives me the credit for his tasteful clothing selections when he could easily say "thank you" to compliments he receives.

Happy couples know each other's strengths and weaknesses. They rely on these strengths in good times and bad. They reinforce these strengths by offering compliments and congratulations when well deserved. Happy couples attempt to strengthen weaknesses by offering constructive and respectful advice or by seeking instruction on how to perform difficult tasks. For example, I am not mechanical at all, so I ask my husband for help with those types of items when they falter, as I prefer to not fix them myself for fear of making matters worse. My husband generally asks me about house-related purchases, our pets' behavior, food choices, or other subject areas I know well. We complement each other for having our own set of unique talents and knowledge. Similar to many happy couples, we also seek out and respect each other's opinions, ideas, thoughts, and feelings.

We have observed happy couples respect each other as equals, despite differences in abilities and skills. They don't roll their eyes and become unnecessarily critical when their partner makes a mistake. They avoid sabotaging their relationship with sexist views or "put downs," such as calling a female spouse a "woman driver." They support and congratulate rather than resent or feel jealous of their partner's competence and successes. They derive pleasure from their partner's drive to excel. These are characteristics that exemplify Beth and Carl's relationship.

Beth and Carl are a highly educated married couple. Carl has an active imagination, and as an engineer, he often thinks about inventions or professional pursuits that interest him. He often stays up late at night working on ideas that have potential for success and riches, or are merely interesting to him. Beth does not think his ideas are going to make them rich, but never discourages his attempts to be creative. She prompts him to concentrate on his job, their house, and the projects she plans for them to share. She never laughs at his quirky efforts to be an inventor. Carl realizes he often wasted time and money following his dreams, but Beth rarely points out that she agreed with his sentiments except for when the cost of his ideas became prohibitive. These best friends plan to be married for a long time to come!

Happy couples take an interest in their partner's passions. They want to meet the mentors and influential people, past and present, who are important to their mate. They want to participate in this process by being a supportive and strong influence in their partner's quest for knowledge and excellence. They attend their partner's important family or work-related events. They encourage their partner to meet their goals. They avoid quibbling about little things or the cold topics (discussed in chapter 4) that have little importance in their overall happiness as a couple.

Making Decisions

When difficult situations arise, or an important decision needs to be made, the happy couple takes the time to discuss their ideas. Each offer and respectfully accept realistic solutions. They write down the pros and cons of each possible decision and outcome. For major decisions or important purchases, they gather information, consult with experts, and finally make their decision together. If they cannot agree on a solution, they may choose to gather more information, table the decision until they can agree, or give the decision making to the spouse who is better trained or knowledgeable of the situation at hand. If the decision fails to produce the results they hoped for, they discuss options on how to resolve the matter so they can move on. Happy couples are able to move past these disappointing events. They avoid bringing the mistakes up again and again in an attempt to blame their partner or themselves for errors in judgment. This brings us to a major relationship hurdle that even happy couples must face: the choice to forgive past decisions and actions that might have hurt the other partner.

Forgiveness

We cannot confuse forgiveness with forgetting an action or event. If one forgives a partner, it does not mean the act will ever be forgotten. In general, happier couples do not usually engage in behaviors that are almost impossible to forgive or forget. These behaviors may include having an affair, chronic dishonesty, betrayal, abuse (be it physical, emotional, or verbal), neglect of a child or a pet, neglect of one's own health, criminal activity, and substance abuse. Other less serious transgressions may include forgetting an appointment, accidentally breaking an heirloom, buying a thoughtless gift, being rude to their spouse, and so forth. Forgiveness means the partner is pardoned for this behavior at this time. Forgiveness does not mean the behavior is forgotten, the partner is not hurt by the behavior, or the behavior will be forgiven if it occurs again in the future. Forgiveness does mean the behavior is pardoned and will not be brought up in the heat of an argument in an effort to further punish the offender. Depending on the seriousness of the behavior, the ability to forgive and move on may be two different things. The partner may choose to forgive, but may be too hurt to resume normal interactions with his or her mate for a period of time. The hurt spouse may decide he or she needs more time before they resume intimate relations or are able to relax and have fun with one another. The hurt party may have lost trust in his or her spouse. In this case, more time and reassurance is needed so the trust between them can be repaired. Now the partner who has caused the hurtful feelings must step up to the plate and strongly assure his or her spouse that the wrongful behavior will not be repeated.

Apologize for Hurting a Loved One

Happy couples tell us they are willing to apologize and take responsibility for their actions when they have done something to hurt their spouse. They understand what they have done to cause their mate to distrust them. They understand why their mate is feeling hurt and angry. They make honest promises to never do the offending behavior again; and they keep their promises.

Forgiving a transgression may require the couple revisit their commitment to each other. We encourage the couples we see in therapy to realize they are committed not just to each other, but to their relationship as a whole. They are asked to realize this commitment is a priority to both of them and not allow minor mistakes to hinder their relationship. Once this is realized, the couple can move on to forgive, but perhaps never to forget.

Say "I Love You" and Mean It

Happy couples are open about their feelings. They are comfortable sharing their feelings and thoughts with each other. It seems newly married couples say *I love you* to each other more often than spouses who have been married for years, if not decades. We have found happy couples feel freer to say *I love you* more often than those couples who are less pleased with their marriages. Saying *I love you* brings an instant smile to the face of a spouse, child, family member, and friend. Saying *I love you* also feels good. I dare say I have not seen too many people who can say these words with a scowl on their faces. Saying and receiving an *I love you* feels wonderful, especially when this proclamation is sincere, and not said to gain favor with someone, or used as an off-the-cuff response during sexual relations. So we advise our happy couples to keep saying *I love you*; it's very good emotional food for the soul.

Consideration and Cooperation

Our happy couples tell us they are very considerate of each other. Being considerate requires that a partner considers or takes seriously his or her spouse's thoughts and feelings before behaving in a certain way. Let's meet Ron who needed to improve his behavior with Liz.

Ron was engaged to Liz for six months when they entered therapy. According to Liz, Ron was a very self-centered individual whose number one priority was Ron. They didn't go anywhere or do anything unless it was Ron's idea. Ron made promises he never kept. He forgot to pick up items he promised to bring home. He called at the last minute to say he could not come over for dinner and flatly told Liz to freeze the meal she took hours to thoughtfully prepare for them to share. He did not call when he promised to do so. He was often late for their dates and rarely apologized for his actions.

Liz was able to name numerous reasons why she loved Ron, but hoped he would become more considerate before they wed. Ron truly loved Liz, but was never called to task for his actions. Historically, due to his charm, good looks, and sense of humor, he was always allowed to slip by without apologizing to anyone, not even to his parents. Ron now had to change his ways or lose Liz. Ron entered individual therapy and relationship therapy with Liz. It took Ron another six months to finally become a more considerate and thoughtful fiancé. In his wedding vows, he promised to "be more thoughtful, considerate, and the man Liz hoped he would become." This was a vow Liz hoped he would keep. Fortunately, they were both determined to continue in therapy to sort out their differences and explore reasons for Ron's challenging behaviors.

Being considerate of a partner must be a daily occurrence. A considerate partner will do the following:

- call on the way to the supermarket to ask if there are any items he needs to buy;
- invite her mate to join her in making decisions that affect both of them;
- arrive on time for appointments;
- call if he will be late and provides a plausible explanation for the lateness;

- inform her mate where she is going, who she is with, and when she will be home;
- pick up after herself, and not leave dirty dishes, clothing, or other items lying around for her mate to put away and;
- always considers his partner's feelings before making a statement or providing an opinion that has the potential to hurt the one he loves. When pressed to do so, he uses honesty, compassion, and gentleness in expressing his thoughts and needs.

Cooperation

Our happy couples cooperate with one another in all aspects of their relationships. In family meetings they create fair chore lists that designate what both partners are expected to do and when the chore must be completed. Individual differences in ability, interest, and availability are considered in assigning tasks to be done. The couple is able to join together to make sure each partner contributes equally in running the household. Finances are discussed, if one spouse has more money available to pay for household expenses, the other spouse may do additional tasks that indicate he is contributing his fair share to the running of their home. Happy couples freely demonstrate their appreciation when their spouse puts forth effort toward a task to which he was assigned. Compliments are freely and often given for a job well done.

Planning Sessions

Happy couples have weekly planning sessions during which time they make decisions on major purchases, how they will spend their vacations, what they will do on upcoming weekends, how they will spend their holidays, when they will get together with family and friends, and other important plans. During these meetings, they will decide when or if they will have children, how many they will have, what kind of contraception they will use, what to name their children, how to decorate the nursery, and so forth. After these meetings they reward themselves for completing their chores or other responsibilities. They may treat each other for dinner, have a pizza party, or rent a movie.

Sharing Power

Happy couples share the power in their relationship. They share decision making in all important aspects of their relationship. One spouse does not assume he must be in charge of the finances, house repairs, or other important decisions. In a happy relationship, both parties are in control. They use their planning sessions or family meetings to discuss issues that require their attention. Happy couples discuss how to enjoy their free time, both together and apart. This may include going to the gym, going out with friends, or volunteering at a local homeless shelter. When an imbalance of power does occur, the happy couple may use their therapy sessions to discuss how to put the balance back into their relationship.

We often see power issues in couples where only one partner works. The other partner sometimes feels she or he must essentially step back and ask permission to spend money beyond what may be allotted for basic household expenses. Happy couples consider themselves in a partnership in which each has an important role to play. The need to ask permission from the working partner is not deemed appropriate as both partners are seen as equal. Ultimately, the roles in a given relationship may be different, but nonetheless are respected.

As we have seen in our therapy sessions, happy couples are considerate of each other during intimate moments. They discuss what each person needs and wants during these moments. They do not use force or guilt to convince a partner to be intimate. They are interested in mutual satisfaction and the individual need for the use of exploration and fantasy during their romantic dates with one another.

Our happy couples realize all couples have issues to discuss both in private and in therapy. They regard their commitment to each other and to their relationship as a solid foundation that allows them to feel secure as they explore ways to augment their strengths and bolster their weaknesses. Our happy couples are in love and focus on that feeling again and again. They reinforce these feelings by complimenting their spouse, and helping them feel cherished and appreciated. Our happy couples share the blame for their problems and don't point fingers at each other for their shortcomings. When there is conflict, our happy couples follow our advice on how to handle these occasions fairly and constructively. Our happy couples share intimate moments and thank each other often for just being in their lives each day.

We thank our happy couples for telling us the secrets to their success. We hope their special techniques are useful to all couples who read this chapter.

Chapter Seven

What Unhappy Couples Can Teach Us

In the previous chapter, we learned what happy couples do to stay satisfied with their relationships. In this chapter, we will discuss what can happen to destroy a relationship. We will learn the warning signs of a relationship that is heading for disaster and how to avoid making the same painful mistakes some of our couples made as they searched for lasting love and happiness.

Games People Play

We have met many patients who felt the need to control their partners. Let's meet Dan and Karen who played an unfair love game and lost.

Dan and Karen were co-workers in a hotel. Although there was a rule to not date fellow employees, our sneaky but careful co-workers couldn't resist. They had an instant attraction for one another. In the beginning, Karen found herself in the proximity of Dan's office several times a day. When he exited his office to use the copy machine, or to attend meetings, he found Karen nearby. They exchanged a few words here and there. Eventually, Karen asked Dan to attend a museum exhibit and Dan accepted the invitation. This started a series of dates that became more serious. Karen and Dan became secret lovers. In order to keep their relationship secret, they avoided each other at work. They never had lunch together or shared quick chats at the copy machine. Within two months, Karen fell hard for Dan. Karen entered therapy to discuss her relationship with Dan. It seemed he was "inconsistent." Karen wanted to spend every weekend with Dan, but instead they got together every two or three weeks. Dan never talked about what he did during the weekends he did not spend with Karen. In addition, Dan never included Karen with his family or friends and found convenient excuses when she asked him to join her when she had activities with her friends.

Dan had difficulty with public affection and rarely allowed Karen to hold his hand at the movies or to and from restaurants. Karen never met Dan's family or friends. He did not want to meet hers either. Karen didn't want to pry, but found Dan quite mysterious. She knew their relationship was taboo at work, but didn't understand why she was kept a secret elsewhere. Her attempts to talk to Dan about his avoidant behavior were unsuccessful. He enjoyed their secret affair but did not want to discuss or open up aspects of his life to Karen.

One day Dan invited Karen over for dinner. While they ate their meal, Dan told her there was someone else. Apparently he wanted to return to an old love interest with whom it ended badly a year ago. He said he was "sorry" and wished Karen a "good life." After a few months, Karen learned that this "old love" was another co-worker whom Dan later married.

Unhappy couples recount stories of relationships that are mysterious. One girl or boyfriend may not know how the other friend feels about her. Introductions to their friend's friends or family members may never happen. Whereabouts of the friend during weekends that are not spent together may remain a mystery. They may hear stories about certain special people in their friend's life but may never learn the identity or the nature of the relationships these people have with their friend.

Many people are involved in relationships in which they do not know how their love interest feels about them. Posing the questions "How do you feel about me?" or "Do you love me?" are difficult for most people. For those with low self-esteem issues, or who are easily intimidated, these questions are almost impossible to ask. Often they fear asking these questions may push their love interest away, or they may appear too needy or clingy. They may also fear knowing the truth, which may be that their love interest isn't truly interested enough in them to make a commitment to the relationship. There are those who are faint of heart and do not want to pry into their love interest's lives. They secretly hope they will be invited in when their love interest is *ready* to introduce them to their friends and family.

It is human nature to *fill in the blanks* when someone does not know important aspects about a potential marital partner's life. To fill in those blanks, they think of creative excuses to explain why they are not told how their love interest feels, with whom he spends his free time, and why he has not introduced them to his family and friends. I remember a *Sex in the City* episode in which the friends were coming up with these excuses to explain the actions of a love interest. The boyfriend of one of the friends found these excuses useless. He simply explained they should stop creating excuses for the boyfriend's lack of interest because the boyfriend was simply "just not into" the friend in question. How simple and easy life would be if people would stop rationalizing why a love interest does or does not do as they desire by using those simple words!

Unhappy couples have taught us that when a love interest is elusive, this person is unwilling to invest in the relationship. A person who is unwilling to state how he feels about a special friend, or how he spends his free time when they are not together may not know how he feels at the time. Or he may not want to hurt or annoy his friend if he thinks her feelings are more serious or intense than his feelings. Despite this fear, we tell our patients they really need to be honest about their feelings. We encourage them to avoid leading on another person, as they would not enjoy this treatment if the situation were reversed.

A love interest who does not wish to introduce his family and friends to the person he or she is dating simply does not want to be in a serious relationship with that person. It could also be that this person has *something* or *someone* to hide from the love interest. He or she may be avoiding the questions that are often asked by family and friends when they are introduced to a new love interest. Nevertheless, the game player is not a sure bet for a love interest. His or her elusive behaviors are a clear indication that a casual friendship is probably all than can come of this relationship. Unhappy couples can attest that those who fall in love with the game player are in a game they will likely lose.

I'm Not Ready for Love

There are many legitimate reasons why someone may not be ready for a serious relationship. Age is a major factor, so is maturity. We tell our younger patients it is a good idea to date and date a lot. In this way, they can learn the traits they truly want in a mate. They can learn what kind of person they are most attracted to and find compatible with their needs, goals, values, and beliefs. Those who are in their teens and are still in school with no viable means of support are better off waiting until they are older and can earn a reasonable living. Those persons who are pursuing a career, and have many more years of education and training ahead of them, may believe they cannot direct their focus in two directions: their career and a love interest. They are often correct in this assessment. It's a good idea to settle into a career path and be more monetarily secure before making a jump to the altar. Marriages that are more stable and therefore happier are those that include people who know who they are, what they want, and where they are going in life before getting married.

In an era of political unrest, many of our soldiers who intend to go overseas may not want a lover to wait for them in case they die in battle or return to civilian life emotionally and/or physically changed. Those who are battling a life threatening disease may avoid love. They may not want their spouses to share their emotional ups and downs as they fight their disease. Ultimately, they may not want their spouses to eventually watch them die.

These are all understandable reasons to put love on hold. Nevertheless, there are many couples who give each other strength during wartime, when a loved one is battling a serious disease, or when a partner is spending twelve hours a day cutting up cadavers in medical school. So it is not a given that one should avoid a serious relationship when pursuing an advanced degree, going to war overseas, or fighting a war within one's own body. This truly depends on the couple's emotional maturity, strength of their love, and their determination to stay together through thick and thin.

Let's consider another situation as we meet Kim and Kenny. Kim and Kenny were high school sweethearts. Their friends and family thought they would marry someday. After high school graduation, Kim entered City College as a biology major and Kenny joined the navy. On a date at the beach, he told Kim he didn't know what he wanted to do with his life and needed to "find himself." Kim found this disconcerting. She knew exactly what she wanted in life. She wanted to marry Kenny, become a marine biologist, live in their hometown, have children, and buy a horse. Kenny asked Kim to "wait" for him, but he couldn't say for how long. It seemed he was expected to say that, but he was not sure that was how he honestly felt about Kim. After participating in this discussion, Kim was suddenly lost, resentful, and sad. Her whole life seemed turned around.

When we met with Kenny and Kim in a therapy session, we asked them to examine their feelings for each other. They both thought they loved each other, and were certainly used to being together. We gave them an exercise in which they were asked to describe how they envision their lives five, ten, and twenty years from now. Kim easily answered this exercise with the life map she had in place: Kenny, career, house in town, children, and a horse! Kenny's responses were much less clear. He wanted to find a career, but did not know what he wanted to do. He could not identify a passion or a career goal he wanted to attain. He also commented that once he chose his career path, he did not know where it would take him, so he was not resigned to remain in the town where he grew up. He thought about marriage at times, but saw it somewhere in the distant future. The thought of having children and a horse seemed well in the future, if at all.

Kim and Kenny resolved they would remain together until life circumstances parted them. Well, life circumstances brought Kenny several states away to pursue training as a fighter pilot. Consequently, they saw each other every few months. Kenny was then sent overseas for additional training. He told Kim to not wait for him as he was scheduled to be deployed and "would be away indefinitely." Kim took his wishes seriously and decided to not put her life on hold even though she would have waited for Kenny if he wanted her to do so. Two years later, Kim married a fellow biologist she met in graduate school.

It is difficult to determine whether one should wait for another to find himself. This can take an indefinite period of time. I advise my patients to focus on what they are currently doing in life. If they are pursuing education, saving for a house, making plans for travel overseas, then do it. I simply say, "do you"; do what is right for you. I advise them to not put their hopes and dreams on hold as they wait for *a spouse in waiting* to decide what he or she wants to do as far as they are concerned. I ask them to consider how they feel about waiting indefinitely for someone who may or may not return to them. If they choose to wait, then they must be prepared to wait for a potential lover who is not ready, willing, or mature enough to commit to a serious relationship. A *spouse in waiting* must be aware of the possibility that their love interest may not want to commit when they have finished their education, tour with the army, and so forth. Both parties must be prepared for the possibility that their love interest may have found someone else in the interim. Of course there are many examples of individuals who were patient, and their patience paid off. So it is a toss up; of course life is a toss up as well. The person who is ready for a commitment has two obvious options: to wait for her love interest or to find someone else who is also ready and commit to him.

Conflicting Emotional Baggage

Some of the couples we met had serious personal or individual issues that clashed. Their unresolved needs and hurts that stemmed from their past made it difficult to essentially move on to a healthy relationship in the present. Let's use Nicki and Mike to illustrate this point. Nicki and Mike had been dating for a year. Nicki was emotionally and physically abused as a child by her alcoholic father. She grew up feeling rejected and "not good enough" in her relationships with men. She had a tremendous need for validation, attention, and affection. Mike had been seriously hurt by a former fiancée just before he met Nicki. He was guarded and wanted to move ahead very slowly with Nicki. He did not introduce her to his friends or family, and he only wanted to go out once or twice a week. Nicki felt insecure in this relationship and made constant demands to be more included in his life. She further often accused him of infidelity since he was not always willing to go out with her. She believed he must be with someone else. She made many demands on how to prove his love for her. Mike grew quite weary of Nicki's demands and accusations. After a series of breakups, Mike finally said good-bye to Nicki.

Mike and Nicki had conflicting unresolved issues that caused their relationship to fail. Each needed time to heal from their wounds before entering into a serious relationship. Each would benefit from psychotherapy to help them better cope with their painful histories and prevent them from carrying their pain into current relationships.

When we meet with couples who have individual issues that affect their ability to relate to others in a healthy manner, we suggest individual therapy together with couples therapy to best treat their individual and relationship issues.

Let's Just Be Friends

Howie met Jane in college. They had many of the same classes and became fast friends. Jane loved Howie's sense of humor. She always found herself laughing when they were together. They shared many friends and enjoyed the same restaurants and hobbies. Howie thought Jane was *it* for him. He thought Jane was gorgeous, funny, and smart. He couldn't ask for more. Whenever they saw each other, they hugged and kissed. Howie wanted to engage Jane in more intimate kisses, but Jane would somehow gracefully pull away.

On Jane's twenty-first birthday, Howie gave her a diamond heart necklace and told her he loved her. Jane blushed as she held the necklace in her hands, but did not offer to put it on. She told Howie that she "just wanted to be friends." She admitted that she *loved* him, but was not *in love* with him. She was attracted to his smile, his generous heart, and his great sense of humor, but somehow felt that he *wasn't her type*. Howie asked for an explanation and received a laundry list of traits her boyfriends in high school had that *attracted* her. It seemed Jane had a type of guy in mind, and Howie didn't fill the bill.

In desperation, Howie tried to become Jane's perfect man. He followed the laundry list of traits she found attractive. He cut his hair, wore a different style of clothes, and got a second job so he would have more money to spend on her. Jane appreciated his efforts, but to her, Howie was still Howie and that just wasn't enough. Jane eventually found her perfect knight in history class and broke Howie's heart.

We have met many patients who, like Howie, were desperate and lost in love. They tried to be someone different, someone who would change their love interest's mind. They thought getting a different hairdo, new clothes, bleached teeth, or a fancy car would somehow transform them into someone new, someone more desirable. Unhappy couples teach us these efforts do not work. Not everyone who looks for a certain type of partner finds their true love. Sometimes they find their idea of an ideal partner is quite different from their original description.

In chapter 5 we discussed compatibility, or that *je ne sais quoi* (I don't know what) that seems to ignite a spark between two people. A new car or a different haircut cannot spark compatibility. It's either there or it isn't. For Jane, Howie did not have that spark, that je ne sais quoi. It is our belief that if a person is told they are not a certain type and are asked to be "just friends," it's better to accept that fate rather than hope to change the person's mind by changing themselves.

We have met many individuals who aim to be the perfect *spouse in waiting*. They truly believe that if they act just right, are the perfect person who is patient and loving in every way, they will be irresistible. The result will be that the person of their dreams will come to their senses and will love them back. This happens in the movies, and perhaps occasionally in real life, but in our experience, it's a long shot. We have met too many people who tried to be the best they could possibly be, and were distraught that their best was not good enough. We explain to these individuals that their best was good enough, but their love interest wanted something or someone different. We explain that good, better, and best have nothing to do with it. Love is not logical. Love is not measured by who is the most patient, the best lover, has the prettiest face, or who cooks the most delicious meals. Love happens when a spark is ignited between two people who just seem to fit together. It is that spark, that special fit that allows them to take those steps toward commitment and intimacy. Jane could not take those steps with Howie. The fit just wasn't there for her. We advise couples to avoid following Howie's footsteps by *putting good effort into either bad or going-nowhere relationships*. Again, we refer to the red flags that must be heeded in every relationship. The red flags are the indicators that something is wrong in the relationship or that the behavior of the love interest is of concern. The red flags must be raised; they must be noticed; they must be addressed; they must be discussed in order to move forward in the relationship. So to all of those who aim to be perfect, we advise to just be yourselves. Your *spouse in waiting* will find you to be just right!

Infidelity

Our couples who enter into relationship therapy are asked to give up their extramarital affairs during this process. We believe having partners outside of a committed relationship negates the effort we are making to strengthen their relationship and to deepen their love and trust in one another. Infidelity breeds distrust and distrust is destructive. Our unhappy couples can verify that trust is extremely difficult to retrieve once it is lost. We therefore ask them to commit to an *integrity agreement*. This is simply stated: *if one partner is interested in dating someone else, they must inform their current partner and leave their current relationship before acting on their desires.* This is a vow not to cheat, and we take this vow very seriously in our relationship therapy sessions.

The exception to this agreement is for those couples who are in *open relationships.* These are couples who may be dating, engaged, or married, but prefer to be open to romantic and/or sexual opportunities with others. Both spouses must agree to this type of arrangement for it to work for them. Yet we believe those in open relationships make an *integrity agreement* to at least tell their partner when they are dating or having an affair with someone outside of their relationship. By sharing this knowledge, the one who is having an affair shows some respect and consideration for his or her spouse. It also alerts the spouse that there may be a health threat to consider. The possibility of passing on sexually transmitted diseases increases with each extramarital affair one entertains.

With that said, we have met many couples who have told us their relationships were torn apart because their partners were unfaithful. Yet many of these individuals continued their affairs despite promises to the contrary. We mentioned trust and how difficult it is to get back once lost. Many spouses feel deeply hurt and confused that the commitment they made in front of clergy, family, and friends was not honored. They feel torn and empty by what they describe as "deceit" and "betrayal." Victims of infidelity often tend to doubt their mates ever loved them, even on the day when they said, "I do." As they process their hurt and disappointment, they may engage in soul searching to determine what they did wrong or could have done better. They may blame themselves for their spouse's infidelity. They wonder if they should have improved their appearance, lost weight, got a better job, kept the house cleaner, learned to cook, and so forth. Their feelings of low self-esteem and inadequacy become destructive as they may even try to essentially compete with their mate's love interest.

Our unhappy couples tell us this competition is not about who has the best figure, car, or career. It's about why the couple stopped making each other happy. It's about why a spouse is seeking a different love interest. It's about why the couple became distant and stopped fully functioning as a couple. It's also about the sadness, grief, and loss of a relationship, and a best friendship in cases where there was once great hope of a forever life together. It is interesting to note that many of those we have met who have been unfaithful to their spouses have been able to *compartmentalize* their behavior. They are able to somehow mentally and emotionally separate their home lives from their extramarital affairs. It seems the person who is able to compartmentalize is also better able to justify or find a viable excuse for his or her behavior. Their two worlds do not collide unless or until their spouse learns of their infidelity. For many spouses, they are able to continue their secret lives for many years or until they were somehow caught by their spouse. When asked why they have not had the integrity to leave their spouse, they often say they did not wish to hurt or disappoint their spouse or children, raise suspicion at work, or were not committed to their outside love interest.

Online Activities

With the advent of the internet, matchmaking sites, chat rooms, and pornography are available to all those who are interested in pursuing these activities. We hear of more and more people who are entering into relationships online. Some of those people consider themselves dating or are friends with those individuals with whom they chat, but have never met.

Sexting, or entering into sexual relationships with online users, is now more common then ever. Sexually provocative language, often coupled with an exchange of equally provocative pictures, is shared online. The question exists, "are online sexting and an exchange of nude pictures considered infidelity if the individuals involved have never met?" Can you be cheating on your spouse with someone you have never touched? Our answer to this question is a resounding *"Yes!"* This behavior represents an attempt at betrayal, as it involves keeping secrets. The question to those who engage in this behavior is, "Would you sext if your partner was at your elbow, thereby observing your behavior?" If the answer to this question is "no," then the behavior is considered cheating on a spouse. If the answer to the question is "yes," then likely the relationship between the spouses is considered open, and allowing of such conduct by both individuals involved in the relationship.

Dishonesty

Few people can tolerate a dishonest partner. I have met many people who lied about everything to the point where no one could tell if what the spouse said was fact or fiction. Some reasons for lying include wanting to impress others, be something or someone different from who he or she is, escape from certain unwanted consequences if the truth were known, to sugarcoat the truth for fear of annoying or losing a significant other, and convenience. For some people it is easier to lie than to tell the truth. A liar sometimes enjoys watching her audience believe her lies. This is somehow a triumph, a coup! Unhappy people who live with dishonest spouses may become numb to the dishonesty. They eventually do not expect to be told the truth, so they stop listening. They say that they do not believe anything they are told, even when told the truth. They complain in therapy of the constant deceit they face. They feel betrayed, disrespected, and undermined by their lying partner.

We advise that spouses confront their mates when they catch them in a lie. We inform them that even if the lying spouse does not change her ways, at least she will know she is not fooling her mate with her lies.

We caution dating persons to think twice and three times before committing their hearts to dishonest individuals. Unhappy couples will attest that these unions rarely last and are not enjoyable. The exception is when the dishonest person truly changes her ways. Even when this occurs, they will not be trusted for a long time as they have the reputation for being a liar. Nevertheless, the person who wishes to change will hopefully someday win back the trust of a loved one.

Secrets

There are those who believe keeping secrets from their spouse is preferable to being open and honest. By doing so, they avoid consequences such as arguments with their spouse, confrontation, buckets of tears, and possible rejection. Yet once the secret is learned, the consequences that were initially anticipated will likely be worse. The spouse who learns the secret reports feeling betrayed by his or her partner. The spouse now has a nagging suspicion that there are indeed other secrets he or she will uncover with more diligence and investigation. Quite often, after uncovering a secret, the relationship is never the same. The trust that once existed between the individuals is tarnished at least temporarily. The only hope for these couples is consistent openness, honesty, and sharing of important information that can affect their relationship.

Temper Tantrums and Abuse

Explosive individuals tend to lose their tempers quickly. They may be intolerant of even petty annoyances, and often "blow up" over inconsequential events. The result is their spouses often feel like they have to *walk on eggshells* and will withhold information from them to avoid their lightening quick tempers.

During a temper tantrum, an individual may shout, throw things, threaten to harm himself or others, or follow through and become assaultive or abusive. The abuse may be physical and result in the person striking out at others in the immediate environment. The person may attempt to harm himself by cutting himself or using a weapon. He may abuse himself with alcohol or drugs. He may attempt to commit suicide. Sexual abuse may result in forced intimate contact and rape. Emotional abuse can result in insults, loud verbal abuse, cursing, or verbal threats to harm others. The temper tantrums may involve destruction of property. Those who are present to observe a temper tantrum feel threatened, even if no physical force is present. The threat comes from knowing that the individual is out of control and anything can happen.

We have observed explosive individuals may feel remorse after the incident and will promise to never lose control again. Their unhappy, frightened mates will cling hopelessly to these promises only to be disappointed when episodes reoccur.

We advise that explosive individuals receive intensive psychotherapy to explore the nature and cause of these events. We have learned from unhappy couples that it is best to avoid getting involved with persons who exhibit threatening behaviors. If these behaviors occur after the commitment has been made, then our advice is to find safe shelter so no one in the house (including children and pets) are further exposed to this dangerous situation. The individual in question will likely need psychotherapy and perhaps prescribed psychotropic medication to assist in extinguishing these behaviors.

Interfering Family Members

Many family members interfere with good intentions. They may want to be helpful or generous. Others interfere to control the lives of those around them. Bill and Jenny had to deal with this type of issue. Bill's family wanted to be helpful to their newly married son and his wife Jenny. Bill's mother and sister were over to their apartment several times a week. They purchased items they thought would look nice, even though Jenny and Bill didn't ask for or particularly want these items. It was a family ritual to spend every Friday night at Bill's sister's house. All holidays were spent at Bill's parents' house, despite Jenny's requests that they spend some holidays with her family or friends. Bill's mother told Jenny what to cook for her son for dinner, what to buy him for his birthdays, and how to take care of him when he caught a cold.

Jenny didn't want to seem ungrateful or rude to her sister-in-law or mother-in-law, but she wished they would stop interfering in her life. One evening she and Bill had an argument. Bill tried to convince Jenny his family members "only wanted to help," and not to take their kind gestures as attempts to control them. Jenny protested and explained that she indeed found their gestures controlling and patronizing. She felt they treated her as if she were a child. She found their constant control and advice disrespectful. Jenny left the house to cool off and Bill immediately called both his mother and sister to tell them about his fight with Jenny. In his attempt for affirmation that he and his family were right and Jenny was wrong to be unappreciative, he formed an alliance with his mother and sister that ultimately left Jenny out. This prompted Jenny to call for a therapy appointment. She felt at a crossroads and was wondering whether she should leave Bill.

When we met with Jenny and Bill, it was clear that Bill was enmeshed with his family and was unwilling to side with his wife for their independence as a couple. He felt he had too much to gain by remaining enmeshed, and that independence from his family posed too great a risk of losing their affection and devotion. He believed "a good wife" would understand the meaning of "family" and appreciate the close bond he shared with them. In therapy we further explored Bill's concern about losing his family's love and devotion and what that meant to him.

We prompted Bill to understand his wife's point of view and the importance of making her a priority in his life.

We have met unhappy couples who were torn between the loyalty they share for their family of origin, and the love they feel for their spouse. We help them to understand their parents and siblings need to adjust to sharing their children and siblings with their new members of their family. Yet, some families find it difficult to change old habits, and many believe the old habits do not have to change at all.

Bill's sister believes Friday night is her time to entertain her family. Bill's mother believes it is her responsibility to teach Jenny how to properly take care of her son, and that she is in charge of all holidays.

Jenny and Bill need to help Bill's family understand their need to create their own traditions and to include Jenny's family and their friends into the mix. Jenny was advised to tell her new mother-in-law that she appreciates her advice and her concern, but she is a good cook, a thoughtful gift giver, and is capable of taking care of her husband when he has a cold. She may add that she would like the opportunity to consult with her mother-in-law when she truly needs her advice in these areas.

Bill, on the other hand, has other issues. He is afraid that if he gains independence, he will lose his family's devotion. He already set up a barrier against Jenny by calling his mother and sister when they had a fight. We inform our couples that it is important to establish a united front as a couple despite recent quarrels and dissention. Bill invited his mother and sister to create a divide or split between his family of origin and his wife. This was a no win situation for Jenny. We never knew the outcome of this case as Bill and Jenny quit therapy after the third session.

Establishing priorities is important for all couples. Unhappy couples do not see their spouses as the main priority in their lives. This is a mistake; the spouse should be the number one priority to his mate. If a spouse cannot consider his mate a priority, then we must explore the reasons for this decision in marital therapy. Simply stated, a couple cannot remain happy if they do not regard each other as number one in their lives. They must understand that on their wedding day, they are telling their family of origin that their spouse and future children are now and will be forever number one in their lives.

Jealousy

The green-eyed monster can be a serious threat to a relationship, especially if it is intense and chronic. Even happy couples can go through periods of minor jealousy when they see their spouse achieve a coveted goal, win an honor, a special promotion, or receive a sizable raise in pay. Jealousy can occur when a mate wins a prize or is given extra attention for a job well done. The jealous partner may feel left out of the limelight in which the mate is basking. The jealousy may be a mask for feelings of low self-esteem or a sense of failure that lies just below the surface of their awareness.

Chronic and intense jealousy is different. It creates a barrier of resentment, which in turn increases anger and distance. When a wife is seriously jealous of her husband or vice versa, she tends to set up an unhealthy competition. The gloves are off and the couple is more prone to fight until someone wins. This attitude negates the spirit of cooperation that benefits all couples. When our couples are jealous of each other, we explore the reasons for these feelings. Individual therapy may be helpful to carefully examine the origins of this destructive influence in their relationship. We hope to determine why these feelings persist, so we can prevent them from destroying the relationship. We repeat to our couples, "It is not a competition, it is a marriage."

Jealousy sometimes occurs when one partner is more popular or attractive to the opposite sex than the other. Those feelings of insecurity are insidious. They can create insecurity in many solid relationships. We repeat to patients that in our society at large there is always someone better looking, better dressed, more educated, more sophisticated, and more confident than they are. Consequently there is always the chance that a more accomplished individual will be attracted to their partner. What they must remember is to not be threatened by this person. We caution these individuals to not make accusations of disloyalty when the mate has been innocent of infidelity. After all, we believe we are all innocent until proven guilty. We encourage our patients to believe their mate is loyal to them and has integrity regardless of who makes passes at them. If the mate lacks this loyalty and integrity, then it is important to further examine this relationship to see if the potential for infidelity exists.

Substance Abuse/Addiction

Many of our couples have described their addictions to cigarettes, drugs, alcohol, sex, or gambling as *their second spouse.* For those individuals, the addiction has taken on a life of its own. It removes the focus from the mate, the children, the house, and the occupation to the addiction. If the mate is opposed to the addiction and tries to rid of the alcohol, drugs, or money spent on gambling, then the mate may feel rejected or left behind. A mate who has

a serious addiction may have difficulty comprehending that they are con-
sumed by the source of the addiction. We have seen couples end their relationships from the strain of seeing their mates lose their jobs and dignity in
search of their next drinking binge or win at the track.

We refer addicted patients to professionals who are specifically trained to
treat the particular addiction. While the identified patient is in recovery, we
continue relationship therapy to help the couple build on the positive aspects
of their relationship.

With the advent of the internet, we have seen many more cases of sexual
addiction in our practice. Other patients report being "addicted" to reading
and studying internet sites, magazines, and books in which the form of the
naked human body is displayed. Many of these patients report they are addicted to pornography that is displayed over the internet. Some visit chat
rooms where sexually explicit conversations and flirtations occur. Our patients describe that orgasm through masturbation is the ultimate goal of these
encounters. Some of our patients have reported they have become more
satisfied with the sexual release they get from their addiction than they do
from sexual activity with their marital partner. Relationship therapy and/or
individual therapy is often recommended in cases where the sexual addiction
becomes the third spouse in the relationship.

Children Who Sabotage Their Parent's Relationships

When a couple separates or divorces, the children are greatly affected and
influenced by their parents' decision. Some children might think the split was
their fault. They reason that if they were kinder, smarter, or somehow better,
their parents would still be together.

A child may observe that one parent is deemed to be "bad" and is asked to
leave or move out. The child may become fearful that he too will be asked to
leave if his parent gets mad at him. These feelings of fear and resentment are
difficult for all children to understand and tolerate, especially if they are quite
young when their parents separate.

So how does a child cope when a parent starts to date someone new? How
do they feel when the new person in their parent's life sleeps over and
attempts to step into a parental role? It is likely the child will rebel and resent
the "new parent" for trying to replace the parent who has left home. What's
more, the child may feel displaced and threatened by the affection and time
spent with their parent's new love interest.

As the child rebels against this new relationship in his parent's life, he
may challenge his parent to make a choice, "It's the boyfriend or me!" The
parent may try to ease the child's feelings and help him feel less threatened
by buying him presents, and spending more time with him. Parents must be
careful to avoid trying to bribe their children with gifts and special privileges.

If the new love interest remains, then so will the child's resentment and efforts to break up the new relationship despite receiving the new bike or later bedtime hours.

Parents must be aware of their child's feelings and do what they can to help the child understand the marriage did not end because of him. Parents must help the child feel secure that although they no longer have two parents who live together, they still have two parents who love them. Further, his parents will not get reunited because the child wants them to be together. With that said, parents must also be careful to not allow their guilt of a broken marriage or an unhappy child influence their decision to pursue or break off with a special and new love interest. After all, this new love may be Mr. or Ms. Right!

Growing Apart

Many of our unhappy couples have reported discontent in their relationships when it appears they have grown apart. They no longer share the same interests, the same goals, or values as they did when they first got married. Perhaps they married at a young age; perhaps they have pursued higher education, or have traveled extensively on their jobs, which caused the growth or change that now challenges their marriage. Of course it can be due to falling out of love, which is not necessarily due to falling in love with someone else.

In therapy, we ask our couples to identify what they continue to have in common. We ask them to name areas in which their spouse needs further growth. We ask the spouse who has stopped growing emotionally or intellectually if he or she is willing to take steps to become more advanced in areas that interest their mate. Sometimes there is willingness to grow together, and sometimes one spouse must say good-bye to the other who prefers to remain unchanged. After all, the changes that may have occurred need not be anyone's fault. They may not be wrong or bad, just merely different. Therefore, separation may be the best remedy for a relationship that has inalterably changed.

Finances

Many, if not most, of our unhappy couples have complained of how finances are handled in their marriage. It is often that one spouse spends too much money and thereby demonstrates a lack of respect for the family budget. Another frequent complaint is that one spouse fails to keep track of their spending by not saving receipts. Others spouses we have met fail to look at the amount of money that remains in their checking or savings account before spending money. Consequently, they frequently overdraw their accounts and bounce checks.

Many of the offending spouses do not tell their partner of their financially negligent behavior. Instead, a spouse may find proof of the mate's financial blunders by doing banking online, or by receiving letters or telephone calls from creditors that their accounts are overdrawn. This issue naturally causes a great deal of tension and dissention, especially if these errors occur frequently, which is normally the case with couples we see. We tell all of our couples that it is essential to plan their budgets and pay their bills *together* on a weekly basis. In general, the initial meetings will take a few hours for the paperwork to be put in order and for the arguments and disagreements to subside. Once financial agreements are made, the maintaining of the budget can be handled quickly, especially if meetings are held on a weekly basis.

Both parties must know the exact amount of money coming into their family, and the exact amount spent on bills, savings, food, clothing, gasoline, as well as miscellaneous expenses and luxuries such as vacations and new cars. Both spouses are reminded to keep all receipts for review. An envelope for these purposes should be kept in a handy location by each spouse. The envelopes are reviewed during the weekly budget meeting.

Selfishness

One chronic complaint made by unhappy couples is that a spouse is selfish. This can mean the spouse only thinks of him or herself when making decisions. This lack of consideration is often the cause of many arguments in unhappy marriages. The selfish individual tends to not think of themselves as *we* or *us*, but rather as *I* in their marital relationship. They typically do not stop to consider what their spouse will say, or how their spouse will feel before making plans or commitments to others. One of the spouses I saw in therapy actually purchased a house without showing his spouse the property he was interested in for both of them.

Selfish individuals fail to do their fair share of household responsibilities. They are difficult to engage in sharing chores or other duties deemed necessary to run a household. They often do not clean up after themselves, leaving coats and shoes on the floor and dirty dishes in the sink. The expectation (that is often met) is that their dutiful spouse will pick up after them.

Many of the selfish spouses we see in therapy claim they were *spoiled* by their parents. They believe they remain entitled to have things done for them. Others claim they "forget" to do the expected chores. Or, they claim they plan to get to the task "later." They later discover their spouse could not wait for the task to be done at some indefinite time in the future, so the task is done for them. The selfish spouse therefore learns if he or she puts off doing a task long enough, it will be done for them. We remind our selfish spouses that they have shared responsibilities in their marriage. They are expected to do their fair share of the chores, take care of their responsibilities, and to pick up after themselves. We advise the creation of chore lists that must be posted for all family members to see. The lists include the name of the task, who is responsible for it, and the deadline for when the task must be completed.

In our sessions we further explore the reason for the selfishness we see. We help the selfish spouse learn to see the world through the eyes of their partner. We help them to gain insight into why they act selfishly and how they must change their ways to achieve harmony in their marriage.

They are reminded that these are the same responsibilities they will some-day teach their children. We advise that it is best that they practice these skills now so they can be terrific models for their children and more considerate spouses for now and forever.

Chronic Criticism

Many of the spouses we see state their mate criticizes them for just about everything. It seems they cannot do anything right. If this behavior becomes chronic, it can take a terrible toll on the self esteem of the recipient of the complaints. As psychologists, we are aware that those who complain excessively are generally unhappy with their lives and most especially with themselves. When we observe the chronic complainer in our sessions, we are prone to encourage this person to seek individual therapy to determine the underlying cause of their chronic discontent. Naturally if the complaints are justified, we must look at the behavior of the person who is receiving the complaints to determine if he or she understands what is causing such unhappiness in their marriage. We want to know if this person lacks understanding of what is expected of her, does not care about the requests that are made to correct the problem behavior, or if their behavior is vindictive or purposeful. We understand some complaints are justified.

In therapy we encourage the person who criticizes others to be aware of what words she uses, her tone of voice, and her body language when she speaks. We encourage her to be constructive rather than destructive in her comments. We advise her to not yell or raise her voice when giving her spouse the feedback he may need to hear. Further, we advise that she not use body language that causes her to appear threatening or defensive.

It is clear that unhappy couples have as much to teach us as those who are happy. Unhappy couples provide a clear example of what not to do in a marital relationship. It seems that couples who are honest and express their goals and expectations early in a relationship are better able to select the right partner. Couples who avoid the pitfalls of committing to a partner who is

abusive, jealous, dishonest, unfaithful, or are simply unready for a relationship also avoid the likelihood of an unhappy relationship and divorce later in
life.

Chapter Eight

Sharing Ideas and Providing Constructive Feedback

We have discussed the importance of compatibility and effective communication skills. We know happy couples often discuss their feelings and experiences with each other. They offer each other support and feedback in a constructive manner. When they have difficulty handling conflicts with each other, they practice the communication and conflict resolution exercises we discuss in chapters 3 and 4. In this chapter, we discuss how to give and receive feedback so it is fair, understood, and respected.

Naysayers

Many people are brought up in a *naysayer* environment. If you share an idea with a naysayer, they are apt to find a problem with it and are quick to point out why it won't work. This is the type of negative atmosphere where the proverbial glass is neither half empty nor half full. Instead, the glass is always empty. There are individuals who are aware of this unhealthy attitude in their parents, friends, co-workers, and spouses. Some individuals are able to overcome it or disregard it so it doesn't become their philosophy of life or a way of interacting with others. There are those who do not consider this attitude negative, rather they consider it realistic. They rationalize that one should never get their hopes up for fear they will be disappointed.

This type of thinking discourages a sense of adventure, a willingness to try something new, or to pursue a challenging goal. Instead, the naysayer instills a sense of doom, as they point out that others can never do anything right and others will likely fail in their attempts to reach their goals. This thinking is destructive as it hurts an individual's confidence and self-esteem. Some people who have been criticized all of their lives become threatened or angry when they get negative feedback from teachers, friends, and their spouses. They may respond to the feedback by ignoring it or denying it because it is too threatening and hurts too much to hear. Others may argue back, as they have grown tired of hearing the negative rants of those individuals who have nothing constructive to say.

If a naysayer is dating, engaged, or married to an optimist, there will be a struggle as each person tries to prove his way of thinking is best. The naysayer feels proud to announce, "See, I told you it wouldn't work." The optimist will hope to prove the naysayer wrong so he can instill some optimism and sense of hope in his negativistic spouse.

GIVING NEGATIVE FEEDBACK

Giving negative or destructive feedback to a spouse may occur when there is a serious disagreement or conflict. An injured or threatened party may want to strike out or verbally attack his mate for making him feel belittled or criticized without sufficient cause. Let's meet Sally, whose criticisms of Stan produced significant problems in her relationship.

Sally and Stan were engaged for six months when Stan's old girlfriend Ann moved back to town. Ann contacted Stan hoping to renew their relationship. Stan informed Ann he was engaged to Sally, but hoped he and Ann could be friends. Ann jumped at the chance to be friends as she hoped that would be an in so they could get back together. Ann invited Stan to have lunch at their favorite café. Stan accepted the invitation. He was curious about what Ann had been doing during the three years she lived in another state. Stan informed Sally that Ann was in town, and that he hoped to renew their friendship. He assured Sally he was not interested in Ann beyond a very casual friendship, but hoped to see Ann for lunch in the near future.

Sally was certain Stan would return to Ann. She wanted to forbid Stan to see her, but was afraid if she did Stan would do it anyway. Sally acted out her anger and jealousy by "nit picking" at everything Stan said or did. She criticized Stan's receding hairline, his failure to get the promotion he wanted at work, his close relationship to his mother, and even his golden retriever, who she thought was too noisy.

Indeed, Sally was a naysayer, and prone to give negative feedback even on a good day. Sally's attitude always bothered Stan, but he thought he could change it once they married and Sally felt more secure in their relationship. Now that Sally was threatened by Ann's presence, her negativistic behavior was worse than before. Sally unwittingly pushed Stan away. In a panic, Sally called for an appointment to discuss the "romantic triangle" in which she felt trapped.

Sally was encouraged to participate in individual therapy to explore the origin of her naysayer thinking and to help her learn more adaptive problem solving skills. Stan was reminded that a "secure relationship" would not likely change Sally's thinking, since the root of her problem goes deeper than their current arrangement. He was further reminded his friendship with Ann was very difficult for Sally; he would have to take Sally's feelings into consideration before deciding to see Ann or any other female friend.

As we learned from Sally and Stan, some individuals use anger and jealousy as a reason to be insensitive and critical. They want to lash out at anyone who threatens their sense of security and their world as they know it. While they are being critical, they may not be aware they are hurting or pushing away their love interest. Their sole intention is to get back at the person who they perceive has hurt them.

In therapy we try to help a couple learn constructive ways to express their hurt so they do not inadvertently destroy their relationship. We also alert them to know when they have crossed the line and were insensitive or too critical of their spouse.

Sally often crossed the line with Stan by picking on everything that was important to him. This included his hairline, job, mother, and, of course, his dog, all of whom Sally was resentful for taking Stan's attention away from her. It is clear that providing destructive and critical feedback can be definite deal breakers. This was certainly the case for Sally and Stan, whose engagement did not survive Ann's return to town.

When we determine the best way to tell a mate they are behaving in an annoying or hurtful manner, it may be necessary to wait until these feelings can be discussed in a rational and fair manner. This means without undue critical remarks aimed to hurt or discount a spouse. We advise that couples do not discuss anything emotionally taxing unless they are calm, have thought about the reasons for their feelings, and have decided how they will approach the sensitive subject. We also advise that the discussion take place in a location where there are few, if any distractions, and when no one is in a hurry. We do not advocate waiting for a long period of time, because the situation may have changed, or the person who is hurt may become more overwhelmed by his feelings over time. Consequently, he may not be able to discuss them calmly and rationally. We suggest discussing the situation or conflict in either forty-five or ninety minutes. This should allow the partners to calm down so a productive discussion can take place. We also suggest the partners do not sit with their anger and hurt feelings for more than a day. It is much better to express these feelings when the incident has occurred so it can be resolved and the couple can move on.

There have been patients who have told us they hold in their hurt and angry feelings until the moment is "just right." They add that they have to wait until they have practiced the dialog they want to have to the point of having memorized their lines perfectly. They become so intent on using the rights words or phrases that they essentially get *stage fright* when the time arrives to vent their feelings. Then they may not know what to say and their feelings come out with destructive or inaccurate statements to support their views.

As stated, the discussion of a sensitive topic calls for a quiet location free of distractions. We also agree it is good to rehearse how to tactfully approach the sensitive subject. Yet the discussion will probably not go exactly as planned, so creating a dialog that one hopes will take place is not the best approach. Instead, we suggest the use of a list of topics and key phrases that need to be aired. In that way, those who get stage fright will have something to help guide them when they get nervous and forget what they wanted to say to their spouse.

Before one decides to give feedback and approach a spouse with a sensitive topic, he is asked to think about *why* he is so hurt or angry. He can consider exactly what his mate has done to provoke such strong feelings. He can also consider what he has done to contribute to the situation and to take responsibility for his actions.

Once the couple has fully examined the situation from both sides, they can assess if they are being fair to each other regarding the feedback they have provided regarding behavior that one or both of them has exhibited. They can decide on a course of action that can mediate and hopefully resolve the situation to their mutual satisfaction.

We recall that Sally criticized Stan because she was jealous of Ann and felt threatened by Stan's friendship with her. Sally's criticisms of Stan had nothing to do with her true feelings about the situation. She was unfair to have criticized Stan for issues that did not pertain to her feelings of jealousy. In therapy she was introduced to looking at her *motives* before criticizing another person. Sally was helped to understand that criticizing Stan's hair, his mother, his dog, and so forth had nothing to do with her anger and insecurity about Stan seeing an old girlfriend.

In therapy we help our patients analyze and understand why they feel they need to give negative or critical feedback to a spouse. We help them to uncover their motives before they say hurtful comments that could severely and permanently damage their relationship.

Taking a Break

During their forty-five to ninety minute break, the angry spouse is asked to try to calm down and rehearse giving feedback statements that are constructive. The partner can also practice using an even tone of voice and making neutral facial expressions and gestures. He can think about his motives for providing feedback, and whether he truly has a valid issue or complaint to discuss. He may consider what else could be influencing his negative thoughts or feelings, and if they are somehow casting a negative shadow on the current situation.

Negative Feedback and Hurt Feelings

We will now meet a couple who used past events to punish a partner. Robin and Jack are a married couple who hoped to retire early. Five years ago, Jack made a stock investment that went badly. He lost five thousand dollars that was earmarked for painting their house. Jack had recently talked to a co-worker who was frequently involved in buying and selling stocks. Jack's co-worker gave him a tip that Jack wanted to consider. That evening, he asked for Robin's input regarding whether they should invest some of their savings on his co-worker's stock tip.

Robin immediately reminded Jack that he "always makes bad investment choices" and he was "out of his mind and an idiot" if he thought she would agree to "such a ridiculous scheme." She added that Jack "made bad decisions in life, just like his brother, and they would never be able to retire early if Jack kept squandering their money like that." Robin asked Jack to call his co-worker immediately and tell him he would not take his "ridiculous stock tip."

Jack was too upset to respond to Robin. He left the house and went for a long brisk walk. Jack was quite shocked by Robin's response to his investment idea. Her comments and harsh tone of voice caused him to feel unfairly criticized. He didn't realize he had been such a disappointment to his wife. He suddenly felt like a failure, which hurt him most of all.

When we meet with couples, we encourage them to give fair feedback to their spouses. Robin's comments to Jack were unfair, untrue, and unnecessarily hurtful. There was no basis for her statement that Jack had "always made bad investment choices." In their marital history, there was only one incident in which they invested and lost money. Robin's doom and gloom comment about their financial future was certainly exaggerated. It seemed out of context with Jack's request for her opinion to buy stock. Robin's reference to the stock tip as a "ridiculous scheme" also insulted Jack. He now felt ridiculous to have suggested this idea and wondered if he truly were "out of his mind" and "an idiot" for considering such a thing. Robin's negative reference to Jack's brother was also unfair. His brother was a hard worker who was financially comfortable, but would never be rich. His financial picture did not belong in this conversation, nor did he deserve to be maligned this way. Finally, Robin's demand that Jack call his co-worker at home to reject his stock tip was certainly something Jack could not comfortably do. He was appreciative of the tip and had thanked his co-worker for his generosity.

In a ten-minute conversation, Robin broke almost every rule for giving appropriate feedback. Her harsh remarks and tone of voice truly hurt and insulted Jack. Her negative and unfair reference to Jack's brother was out of line. Finally, her demand that Jack call his co-worker to reject his stock tip put Jack in a terribly awkward situation with both his wife and his co-worker. Robin's feedback caused a tremendous rift between herself and her husband. He felt battered and punished by her comments. This episode prompted Jack to call us the very next day.

In our meeting with Robin and Jack, we were interested to learn the reasons why Robin felt so negatively toward Jack. We reviewed their relationship history and learned Robin always wanted to marry a man who could financially support her so she would not have to work. She was angry Jack did not make enough money and she needed to work to help pay for their mortgage, their children's education, and so forth. She was angry at herself for not "marrying up" so she could have a more leisurely life. This anger developed into a deep resentment that seemed to surface whenever the topic of finances was brought up.

Our goal was to help Robin understand her anger and resentment toward herself and toward Jack. We also discussed how to give feedback to Jack without insulting him or hurting his feelings. We reviewed their conversation about the stock tip and provided our own feedback on how the conversation could have been more constructive and respectful. Here are some tips we provide to our couples on how to give constructive feedback.

GIVING POSITIVE FEEDBACK

Stay with Today

When giving feedback, keep in the present. Avoid going to the past to rehash past hurts, mistakes, and disappointments. Robin had brought up a five-year-old investment mistake that did not need to be mentioned in their recent conversation.

Be Accurate with the Facts

Know the facts before giving an opinion. Be open to say, "I don't know, let's find out what we should do." Instead, Robin rejected Jack's current investment idea without requesting they get an expert's opinion on the matter. When in doubt, do your homework, conduct a research study, and get advice. After doing these steps, you can make an informed decision.

Give a Compliment

Sometimes we forget it is a compliment to be asked for advice or feedback. It is apparent someone values our knowledge and opinions. With this in mind, it is helpful to thank the person for valuing your advice. A compliment could also consist of telling the person it is obvious they have thought about the issue a great deal and the issue is important to them.

Be Specific about the Request for Feedback

When someone asks for advice, they may have a specific question in mind. When in doubt, ask them to restate their question. There is an old saying about asking someone for the time and in return getting an explanation of how a watch works. A person may not want to know how you feel about the *entire* situation or subject matter. Perhaps he just wants to know your reaction to one part of it. It is important to ask for clarification so your advice isn't too general or covers ground your spouse would rather not explore with you. When being specific, it is also important to avoid making sweeping statements or judgments about the person who is requesting the advice. Robin stated that Jack "always made bad investment choices." This global statement was simply not true. So it is important to avoid making these harmful generalizations about another person.

Avoid Jumping to Conclusions

Robin was quick to assume the current stock tip was going to fail. She believed all stock tips Jack suggested would fail, based on one negative experience. Experience is a good teacher, but it is essential to know all the facts before making a judgment about the potential success or failure of a pending project.

Stay Focused on the Topic

In order to make a point, many spouses refer to unrelated topics or bits of information that are not relevant to the subject matter or issue being discussed. This results in a diluted discussion in which an accurate or helpful conclusion cannot be reached. We advise our couples to be specific about the topic being discussed and to avoid changing the topic or bringing irrelevant information into the discussion. We also advise our couples to only discuss those individuals who are relevant to the discussion. Robin introduced Jack's brother into their discussion. She wanted to further insult Jack by comparing him to his brother, whom she apparently dislikes. The topic that was up for discussion was whether to consider the stock tip, not Jack's brother's financial status.

Play Nice

We naturally encourage our couples to be kind, respectful, and considerate of each other. We remind each spouse to use a calm tone of voice and avoid gestures and facial expressions that are demeaning or insulting. This includes eye rolling, finger pointing, and raised voices. We also suggest that the person requesting the feedback not be ridiculed for asking for advice. We repeat, it is a compliment to be asked for feedback. Use of cursing or name-calling only serves to hurt and humiliate the spouse who is asking for input. Negative feedback turns the discussion into an adversarial event. When Robin referred to Jack as an "idiot," and "out of his mind," she unnecessarily hurt his feelings and potentially turned their discussion into an argument.

Know Your Motives before Giving Feedback

It is possible to have a hidden agenda when giving feedback. Perhaps it is a desire to hurt the person for an unrelated issue. It may be "pay back time," or "I'm going to reject your idea the way you rejected mine last time we debated an issue." We advise that our couples take time to consider their motives and intentions before sharing their opinions. This may require that a spouse ask for a given length of time to think before giving advice. We originally suggested taking forty-five to ninety minutes before engaging in a difficult discussion. At times it may be preferable to take more time if there is a need to gather additional facts and information.

Try to Be Helpful

We mentioned it is a compliment to be asked for advice. We suggest that when asked for feedback to try to be as helpful as possible. Consider how you would feel if you were being paid for the advice. A professional consultant must be thoughtful and consider the question carefully before giving his advice. His customer wants a considerate and thoughtful response that requires knowing the facts. The customer wants a rational approach free from emotional baggage or hidden agendas. So when giving feedback, it is helpful to take your job seriously and give the best input you can to your spouse.

Keep Expectations and Demands Reasonable

Robin expected Jack to phone his co-worker to say he would not follow his stock tip. This was an unreasonable expectation. It is important to keep in mind that when offering feedback, the receiver has the option to follow the suggestion or reject it. Jack's co-worker was not expecting a response to his stock tip advice. He was merely passing on what he thought was a good deal. Jack knew a call to his co-worker was out of place. In addition, he knew his co-worker would be insulted if he called to reject his advice.

Stay Sober

When asked for feedback, it is important to be sober and not under the influence of alcohol or drugs. These substances cloud thinking and can cause emotional deregulation. It is important to remember that the person who is seeking advice wants a clear and thoughtful response. They want their spouse to stay calm and focused. Substance use or abuse can have a negative effect on these abilities.

Golden Rule

It is important to give feedback to others, as you would like them to give it to you. This means with fairness, consideration, and respect. Nothing less will do.

As we reflect on Robin and Jack's interaction about the stock tip, we are keenly aware they have many issues to work on in their marriage. It is so easy for our unhappy couples to be confused about their relationship issues and allow them to spill over from one situation to another. We instructed Robin and Jack on how to provide fair and useful feedback techniques as already mentioned in this chapter. We wish them success as they continue in therapy.

RECEIVING FEEDBACK

As we consider the role of feedback in our lives, we are aware that sometimes we are the giver and sometimes we are the receiver. We know it is important to be gracious when *giving* feedback. It is also important to be gracious when *receiving* feedback as well. Let's meet Dan who needed some advice on how to receive feedback.

Dan and Minna were dating for the past six months when we met them in our office. Dan was in a difficult period in his life, a crossroads of sorts. He was graduating from college with a degree in engineering. He was considering various career options. He thought about going to graduate school but was eager to enter the work force and earn some "real money." He had a few interesting job offers to consider. He also thought about joining the armed services. Minna was two years older than Dan and was employed as a history teacher in a local high school. Her career choice came easy to her. She loved history and always knew she would become a teacher. Her parents were teachers, so were her three older brothers. Dan often asked Minna for advice on what career path to follow. Minna considered his options, and in her levelheaded way, tried to give him good feedback on his career choices. Dan respected her intelligence, but felt defensive when she offered him advice. He didn't think she understood how difficult it was to make a career choice. He tended to snap at her and accused her of "having it easy" and of "not being able to relate to someone with real career options." He would get so defensive that he sometimes read a magazine while Minna answered his request for advice. One time he shouted at her, called her "a jerk," and left her house. Minna was bewildered and wondered what she said that could have caused him to feel so angry. She also wondered why he would ask her for advice, and then either reject the advice or ignore her when she responded to his request. None of this made sense to Minna.

Minna didn't realize how resentful he felt about the ease with which she was able to make her own career choice. She knew he might move to another state or even out of the country if he joined the army. She felt in a quandary about their future as a couple if he was ordered to relocate. Minna called our office to schedule a session for herself and Dan. She wanted to know how to respond to Dan's request for advice on his career options. She was convinced she was doing something wrong and wanted to make things right with him.

We discussed various aspects of Dan and Minna's relationship. We asked them how they felt about each other and whether they thought they would be together in the future. Both stated they hoped they would be together, but Dan clearly resented Minna's "homespun" way of looking at the world. He felt she didn't understand how he felt about making the right career choice. He also knew that some choices would involve a move and he worried about what that would do to their relationship. After all, he knew Minna was happy with her location and her job. All of these feelings prompted him to be defensive, rude, and inconsiderate when she gave him advice, even though he originally asked for her input. We gave Dan the following advice on how to graciously respond to feedback.

Avoid Being Defensive

Dan resented Minna for having an easy and satisfying career choice. He accused her of not understanding his position and of not having had a "real career choice" to make. He also tried to belittle her chosen career. When responding to feedback, it is important to respect the advice giver and not get defensive or insulting. If a person feels another's frame of reference is too different from his own, then he should not ask for their advice. Nevertheless, it is always polite to say "thank you" for the input given, even if it is not useful.

Take It under Consideration

A polite way to respond to feedback that may or may not be beneficial is to state you will think about it. During this process, you can ask for more information or a clarification of their ideas. Allow the person time to state his views and check with him to see if you understand his advice correctly. Sometimes a restatement is helpful when trying to clarify a partner's stand on an issue. Take notes while receiving feedback and review them at a later date. The information may make more sense after having a chance to quietly reflect on it.

Understand the Other Person's Frame of Reference

Dan thought Minna did not understand his circumstance, so he quickly dismissed her input. It is possible that by listening attentively and asking for a partner's ideas, one can look at a situation from an entirely different perspective. This different perspective can sometimes offer a fresh new way of looking at a difficult issue.

Ask for More Information

Sometimes we reject feedback based on insufficient information. It is always helpful to ask for more information including a partner's rationale for giving certain feedback. It is okay to ask where the partner got her information. It is appropriate to ask where or from whom you can get additional information that will help you make your decision.

Be Self-Reflective

It is important to look at your reactions to others when they provide feedback. We recommend a partner reflect on his reasons for being defensive, negative, or perhaps too willing to accept feedback. It is important to be honest with yourself when assessing your reactions to others.

Avoid Disappointment

We advise that couples not be disappointed with the feedback they receive from others or each other. It is helpful to realize feedback stems from a person's opinion. Their feedback is not necessarily true, false, or a fact. Feedback is only a suggestion; it is not a directive. Therefore, feedback can be graciously accepted or politely rejected.

Avoid Withdrawing from the Advice Giver

Sometimes when Minna offered an opinion, Dan read a magazine or walked out of the room entirely. This was rude and very insulting to Minna who was trying to be helpful. We advise that when a person feels overwhelmed by the advice or feedback they receive, it is reasonable for them to ask for a forty-five to ninety minute break from the conversation. After this period of time, the participants in the discussion can respond to the feedback in a calm and respectful manner

Stay Focused

It is always helpful to stay on the topic being discussed and to only bring up information that is relevant to the discussion. The introduction of irrelevant information serves to dilute the discussion and prevents or inhibits effective problem solving from taking place.

Avoid Taking Advice Personally

People often feel belittled or criticized when offered feedback. They may take revenge by verbally or physically attacking the person who gave the feedback. This approach does not accomplish anything except to create distance and anger between the two parties. If a person feels unduly criticized or attacked, he can ask for his partner's rationale for giving the advice. He can also add that he feels hurt by the feedback that was given and add that he may need a time out to consider what has occurred during this difficult discussion.

Omit Poor Excuses

We know children are great at coming up with excuses for their behavior. We have heard the excuse "The dog ate the homework," or "My brother ate the cookies, not me." When adults attempt to use poor excuses to explain their conduct, it is usually not well received by others. Honesty is always the best course to follow. Deflecting the truth will only make matters worse. Some children may not be able to see through a poor excuse, but many adults are able to tell if a spouse is avoiding the topic being discussed by giving a poor excuse that is transparent to all involved.

Sharing the Blame

An equally childlike response to feedback is to deflect the blame and state "We both misunderstood," or "I think we are both to blame for this situation." Of course this may be true, but when receiving feedback, it is never fair play to place blame on another partner and divert the focus of the issue onto them. Some persons are expert at deflecting blame on others in an attempt to avoid taking responsibility for their own behavior. This behavior is never well received by others.

Golden Rule

Listen attentively to others as you would want them to listen to you. Make eye contact with the individual that is speaking. Respond appropriately to the information and ideas that are shared.

As we review the principles of both giving and receiving feedback with our couples, we are encouraged that they can improve their communication and interaction with each other by following the advice outlined in this chapter. In our day-to-day interactions with others, we cannot avoid either giving or receiving feedback whether it is at home, at work, with our friends, family, or neighbors. We must remember to be fair, polite, and reflective about the feedback offered. We have much to learn and much to offer others in all of our interactions with them. When conflicts arise, we recommend reviewing chapters 3 and 4, where we discuss strategies for positive communication skills and effective conflict resolution.

Chapter Nine

Setting Goals and Meeting Expectations

Each time we meet with a couple in therapy, we ask them to tell us about their previous week. We want to know about any noteworthy events that occurred in their lives and how they handled the situations that arose. As we see improvement in their ability to use positive communication skills and effectively handle their conflicts, we inform them of the skill areas in which we have noted an improvement and the areas that continue to need more work. We ask our couples to assess how they are doing in the marital therapy program. We want to know if they are following the program we have outlined for them. We ask them to describe areas in which their relationship has improved and areas that remain unchanged. Sometimes the spouses will disagree on the extent of their progress. One partner may believe he is doing better than his spouse. When this occurs, we ask each to define what "better" means to them. Sometimes the progress they want to attain is unrealistic after just a few sessions. We often essentially check in with our couples to ascertain what they plan to accomplish in therapy and in their relationship in general.

This brings us to a discussion of goals and expectations. Some goals and expectations for positive growth are fluid and therefore possible to change during therapy. Others are more static or fixed. They may take additional time to change. As we progress in therapy, we discuss whether their goals and expectations are realistic. We help our couples amend those that need to be adjusted, while we work to reach the goals that are more realistic.

Goals and expectations are different concepts. Goals are what each spouse wants to accomplish, whether it be in therapy, in the next week, month, year, or in life in general. They may be specific, such as "retire in Florida by age sixty," or more general, such as "attain spiritual fulfillment in my life."

Expectations are usually what one hopes will happen, such as "to receive a bonus at work in the coming year." An expectation can also be what one person hopes another person will do as well. A parent may *expect* his children graduate from college. A husband may *expect* his wife to remember his next birthday. Expectations are often related to *needs*, which we will discuss in depth in chapter 11.

As we discuss goals and expectations with our couples, we notice many of them have not been shared with each other. Yet we find that many spouses believe their significant others will somehow intuitively know what their expectations are. I wish I had a nickel for each time I heard a spouse state, "After being married for a number of years, you should know what I want for my birthday," and so forth. Many of our couples state that the first time they approached subjects such as what they want in life, plan to do after retirement, and hope to accomplish in life in general, was in our sessions together. We find this very interesting and important to know when working with a new couple.

We encourage each couple to be up front with their goals and expectations from the start of their relationship. We want them to start sharing this information when they are dating, so when they become engaged or married these goals and expectations are not a surprise.

We recall a recent conversation with a couple who had been married for four years. One partner did not know her counterpart intended to return to school for an MBA! This sparked many hours of conversation about what each hoped to attain in life and reasons why this information was not previously shared.

So you can see from this example it is vitally important to regularly share both small and large goals as well as expectations with a partner early in a relationship. When first involved in a relationship, it is important to know as soon as possible if these goals and expectations are compatible. It is possible one person's goal will interfere with another person's expectations. For example, consider the spouse whose *goal* was to return to school to earn an MBA. His plan was to go to school fulltime and his *expectation* was that his wife, a successful pediatrician, would financially support him during this process. The wife was dismayed by this plan, because her *goal* was to start a family, and work part-time so she could be with her new baby. She *expected* her husband to continue working as a CPA so she could reduce her hours at work. She reasoned that her plan would save them money on day care expenses.

As you can see, their goals and expectations were quite different. We discussed their goals and expectations at length in several therapy sessions. The resolution reached was to start a family within two years, or after the husband received his MBA. Fortunately they were both young and healthy enough for the delay to start a family to not be a problem. They were able to arrive at a mutual goal so each of them would be able to support each other's hopes and dreams!

Although a couple's goals and expectations are often related, we will discuss them separately and begin our discussion on *goals.*

DEFINING OUR GOALS

The challenge in defining our goals is to be aware of what they are. Many individuals do not think about having specific goals in their lives. When we ask our patients what they would like to accomplish in the next six months, a year, five years, and so forth, many simply do not know what to say. They get up in the morning, begin their routine, and go about their day in a methodical way. Each day begins and ends the same. They often tend to postpone thinking about their goals until a life event forces them to think about their future. They don't realize their future is now and putting off plans for attaining hopes and dreams is waiting far too long.

Goals Can Be Divided into Different Categories

- Personal goals, or goals each person makes for himself
- Personal goals one partner makes for another
- Relationship goals, or goals a couple makes for their lives together
- Daily goals, or those activities one hopes to accomplish in a twenty-four hour period
- Weekly goals, or those activities one hopes to accomplish in a seven-day period
- Monthly goals, or those activities one hopes to accomplish in a given calendar month
- Yearly goals, or those one hopes to accomplish in a given twelve-month period
- Life goals are those one hopes to accomplish before death

Personal Goals

These are goals one makes for oneself. Achievement of these goals may or may not involve someone else. Examples of personal goals include losing or gaining weight, writing a book, getting together with an old friend, taking a cooking class, painting a room, getting a college degree, quitting smoking, and so forth.

Personal Goals One Partner Makes for Another

It is vitally important that these goals are made with the spouse's awareness and consent. These goals may be daily, weekly, monthly, or yearly. They may include to say "I love you" every day, to mow the lawn every Saturday morning, to quit smoking by next month, or to learn to dance by their wedding next year.

Relationship Goals

These are goals a couple makes together for themselves. These can include having children, buying a house, going on a cruise, taking up golf, building a porch, retirement in Tahiti, and so forth. Happy couples are eager to create these goals and set them in motion.

Daily Goals

These are activities that can either be started and completed in one day, or begun on a certain day, but may take months to complete. A goal of doing a load of wash can be easily completed in one day. Beginning a diet program can begin on a specific day, but may take months to reach a certain goal weight. The ultimate goal of weight loss can include many daily goals that relate to a strict diet and exercise plan. For example, daily goals of walking five miles a day and eating certain foods for breakfast, lunch, and dinner are aimed toward losing a certain amount of weight each day, week, month, and so forth.

Other daily goals include saying "I love you" to your spouse before leaving for work, giving a child a compliment for cleaning his room, reading a chapter of a book, returning a phone call, cooking a meal, or sending a card to a friend.

Weekly Goals

A weekly goal can be getting through an entire work week without losing your temper, painting a room, doing your taxes, cleaning out the garage, planting an herb garden, going on a regularly scheduled romantic date with a boyfriend, refinishing the living room floor, learning a new dance step, or getting the house ready for a party.

Monthly Goals

Monthly goals may include losing ten pounds, getting pregnant, buying and selling a new car, saving up for a lawn mower, visiting a friend who lives three hundred miles away, planning a block party, learning to ride a horse, or getting the boat ready for the summer season.

Yearly Goals

Goals made on an annual basis may include finding a new and satisfying job, moving out of state, going to Europe for a vacation, adopting a child, getting married, preparing for a daughter's wedding, hand crocheting a king-size quilt, planning a fun anniversary celebration, or retirement to a farm in the Midwest.

Life Goals

These are goals one hopes to accomplish in a lifetime. Some of these goals may be specific, others more general and difficult to define. Life goals may include financial well being; a happy marriage; happy, healthy children who have families of their own; a comfortable home; good health; spiritual oneness with God; a satisfying career; few regrets; and a peaceful existence.

Whether the goals are personal or pertain to a relationship, whether they take a day to complete, a year to plan, or a lifetime to accomplish, we recommend you start to make them today. The first way to start a goal is to identify what you want to achieve, and whether you want to do the task alone or with your spouse. If the task involves a mate, then check to see if the goal is mutual or compatible. Work together in therapy or alone to establish goals each spouse finds satisfactory. Identify the steps needed to complete the goals.

It is very important to notice that ones goals have changed. As we mature, we may find our preferences change as well. It is important to inform those who are close to us of these changes of heart. It is also important to ascertain the reaction of these changes on loved ones. Everyone who is close to the one making important life changing goals may be affected by those changes as well.

CREATING REALISTIC EXPECTATIONS

We develop our expectations of others when we are very young. As children, we expect our parents or guardians to keep us fed, clothed, and protected from harm. We expect they will bathe us when we are dirty, give us medicine when we are sick, and comfort us when we are afraid. As we get older, our expectations, as well as our needs, change dramatically. As adults, we no longer need someone to help us put on our pajamas. We can go out and buy our own medicine when we are sick and make chicken soup to help us feel better when we have a nasty cold.

Each one of us establishes expectations based on our early social environment. Our family upbringing helps us to create our expectations regarding the type of persons we want to date and the one we choose to marry. Our immediate and extended family shares their set of values, behaviors, and religious beliefs with those who are close to them. There are certain practices and mores that derive from national origin, religious beliefs, as well as those from the cultural milieu that exists in ones neighborhood or town.

Our expectations regarding what we consider to be appropriate social interactions often stem from our early experiences with our families or guardians. Those expectations may either clash or correspond with the ones we develop from our interaction with friends, neighbors, and the media. We tend to be greatly influenced by what we watch on television, as well as what we read in print. We develop expectations based on our social histories or past experiences with others in our environment. We are also influenced by the experiences and advice given to us by others in our social circle. The major influences in our lives include the following.

Family upbringing and values

This relates to the way family members interact and their social history as an immediate as well as extended family. It includes many things such as the way they celebrate holidays and other special events. The family decides who cooks the Thanksgiving turkey year after year and how they celebrate birthdays, marriages, and other special occasions. The family establishes norms and expectations regarding how one is supposed to dress. They decide what is appropriate regarding the consumption of food and drink. One learns to expect whether particular family members love to eat dessert and other goodies, or only eat healthy snacks to prevent weight gain or diabetes. Some families enjoy serving cocktails or wine when they have visitors, while others abstain from drinking alcoholic beverages of any kind. Some families maintain the cultural mores of their country of origin even though they no longer live in that country. Of course as stated, religious customs and beliefs can be influential in setting the tone of what is expected during certain holidays, martial ceremonies, the upbringing of children, and so forth.

A family often sets an expectation of how others are supposed to interact when they get together for an event or merely for dinner. A gregarious person would feel out of place or be looked at with rejection in a group of quiet and reserved individuals. Families also set expectations regarding how they spend leisure time. Some families go on lavish vacations and must fly first class. Other families are more conservative with their money and may prefer less expensive adventures closer to home.

A couple, be they dating, engaged, or married must consider their family histories and expectations to determine whether they are willing and/or able to create their own traditions, or whether they must follow those that belong to their family. If an individual's family traditions and expectations are not compatible with those of his spouse, then the couple must decide how to create a balance so no one feels ignored or disregarded. They must honestly explore their expectations and experiences regarding many factors already mentioned as well as their attitudes toward marriage and divorce, how big a family to have, their philosophy toward childrearing and sexual expression, whether they require a mate from a given ethic group, religious affiliation, or national origin, what type of jobs or professions are considered appropriate, and so forth. They must also discuss how to handle family expectations they cannot meet. Many of our couples describe the stress of the holidays when they are expected to spend most of their time with one or both sets of in-laws. The competition that exists in families and the need to please everyone can cause many arguments. One set of in-laws may assert much pressure to be chosen as the better place to celebrate certain holidays. We observe much stress in couples where one spouse firmly believes that his or her parents should be visited more often than the parents of the other spouse.

It is important to sort through all expectations to determine which ones are realistic and those that need to be discarded. It is essential to check out the facts about a future spouse before having an expectation that will never be realized. You will now meet a couple that had expectations that were not realistic.

Mary was from a cold and distant family. They rarely ate meals together and birthdays were treated as just another day. Mary longed for a spouse who was from a close and affectionate family. When Mary became engaged to Ted and met his parents and siblings, she thought she had found the perfect family with whom to celebrate holidays, invite over for dinner, and call on the phone just to chat. Ted tried to warn her that his family was a competitive and driven group of individuals who made a good first impression, but failed to follow through on their promises to "get together more often," "buy season's tickets to the Orioles home games," and so forth. He stated they were not often available to attend many family gatherings because they were too busy pursuing their demanding careers.

Mary was terribly disappointed. She made a false assumption about Ted's family and ignored Ted's warnings that they were not the warm and cozy group she insisted they were when she first met them. Ted tried to help Mary understand all relationships have issues and no relationship is perfect. Further, if she was looking for the perfect in-laws and close knit family, then she would not be happy married to Ted. Indeed, Mary worked hard in therapy to change her expectations of Ted's family. Instead, she and Ted worked to create their own family that would share close ties and heartwarming traditions with one another.

It is important for individuals to make their expectations clear when they first become a couple. They must try to avoid making false assumptions or to accuse a spouse of failure or wrongdoing simply because he or she did or did not do something that was based on unrealistic expectations or perhaps a fantasy.

Religious Traditions

Many people are brought up in a particular religion that is practiced by their parents or guardians. Each established religion includes certain customs and traditions. Many families have expectations regarding how these customs and traditions are supposed to be carried out. The traditions may include how to celebrate certain important holidays, the celebration of the birth of a child, religious studies that children are expected to master, how to conduct a marital ceremony, the ceremonies related to the death of a friend or relative, and who is permitted to officiate at religious ceremonies. There may be expectations that the wife is a virgin before marriage and various customs related to sexual habits and behavior. Other expectations may include the act of gift giving and receiving. This may pertain to what gifts are appropriate to give and when the gifts are to be opened. Religious traditions include when, where, and how often family members attend services, who is expected to attend these services, and very importantly, how others are treated if they do not share the same beliefs and customs espoused by the family. We will now meet a couple who clashed due to different expectations regarding how they planned to practice their beliefs.

Claire and Joseph were both of the Jewish faith. They were engaged to marry in six months. Joseph was brought up in a nonreligious family where prescribed traditions were not followed. Claire, on the other hand, attended a conservative synagogue and intended to keep a kosher home, just the way her mother and grandmother had always done. When Joseph and Claire tried to get their families together for Friday night *Shabbat* dinners, they encountered difficulties. Claire's parents would not eat at Joseph's parents' home because they were not kosher. Joseph's family disliked eating at Claire's home because her parents often made comments about their nontraditional beliefs.

As they approached their wedding date, Claire and Joseph experienced increased pressure from their individual families. Suddenly Claire was expressing her expectations that Joseph become more religious after they get married. She wanted him to regularly attend her synagogue and to become kosher, not only in their home, but when he was having lunch at work or out with friends and family.

It was clear that Claire's religious expectations were not expressed until just before the wedding. This was a bit late in the game to expect that Joseph change how he expresses his beliefs and what foods he should eat. Joseph considered Claire's expectations but decided they were unrealistic. He correctly felt she was imposing her values and beliefs on him. They both decided to postpone their marriage to further explore if their expectations and beliefs were compatible.

We advise that couples express their expectations about religion early in their relationships. The goal is to determine how each person's religious beliefs will impact their relationship, both at that time, and in the future. If these expectations are not expressed, the result could be a broken relationship and a broken heart.

National Customs and Mores

In the United States, we have national holidays such as Thanksgiving, the Fourth of July, Memorial Day, Columbus Day, Martin Luther King Day, President's Day, and many others. We have customs that many Americans follow in celebration of these events. Indeed, many other countries have their own national events and customs that family and friends may choose to observe. National customs and mores often play a role in deciding how marriage ceremonies are conducted and family customs are created. Some families are more conservative about these traditions. They may expect their grown children to join them in celebration of these customs. Other families encourage their children to establish their own way of observing holidays. Nevertheless, it is important to understand and respect the expectations of those from various cultures and religions. At times the traditions and customs will help clarify who is compatible and has the best opportunity to spend their lives together with blessings from each spouse's family and friends.

Influence from the Media

We are all aware the media (television, movies, theater, internet, books, magazines, and advertisements) have a tremendous influence on our expectations of others and of ourselves. We know the depiction of perfect families on television often does not reflect the way real families interact. The media has a tendency to create standards many people cannot achieve, and yet the media presents them as if they were attainable by all of us.

When we look back at classic television shows such as *The Donna Reed Show* and *Father Knows Best*, we are aware of the near perfect compassion and warmth the family members expressed toward one another. When people compare their family interactions to those on idealized television shows, they are often disappointed and feel cheated. They cannot expect to replicate the warmth and closeness the characters portray on these television shows with their own family members.

The media also influences the way we believe we are supposed to look. We see perfectly coifed stars and models that we assume represent the norm. When we watch the Academy Awards, we witness a virtual parade of actors who are wearing clothing and jewelry costing thousands of dollars. Practically each one who walks the red carpet has a finely sculpted body that is probably achieved by spending countless hours in the gym each week. In addition, these individuals may have staff including a personal trainer, professional chef, make-up artist, and hair stylist who are at their beck and call on a daily basis. When we see these *perfect* human beings we may aspire to look just like them. We seek an ideal without the benefit of a staff that is present to count every calorie we eat and paint our faces with utmost care and precision.

The recent advent of reality television shows and their emphasis on extensive plastic surgery sometimes creates the illusion that the creation of perfect D-cup breasts is treatment for a patient's low self-esteem and unhappy love life. Other reality television shows such as *The Bachelor* fuel fantasies of what characteristics one should look for in a mate. This show has taught us it is essential to look perfect in a bikini to be eligible for smoldering evenings in a hot tub or playful days on the beach. What we have not learned from shows of this kind is how to create a lasting relationship by getting acquainted with a future partner in a genuine lifestyle that does not include limousines, private planes, and expensive champagne.

When we spend our evenings and weekends watching television, movies, or sporting events, we tend to compare ourselves to the stars of these shows. Most of us fall short of the standard they portray, but our expectations to be in their league causes many people to feel disappointed in themselves. For those who are truly impressionable, starvation diets, extreme plastic surgery,

and holding out for the perfectly groomed mate can have negative consequences. We will now meet Beth and Andy who went to extreme measures to
live up to a media ideal.

Beth was always a bit chunky as a child and teenager. She often dieted to
lose extra pounds "of baby fat," only to quickly gain them back. Beth was
told she "had a pretty face," but her weight interfered with her appearance. In
high school, she never thought she could measure up to the girls in the "in
group." They were the cheerleaders with perky smiles and pretty figures.
Beth went to all the football games and watched the cheerleaders tumble in
the air. She noticed with sadness that none of them needed to lose weight and
many could eat whatever they wanted without weight gain. After the games
the pretty ones with the perky smiles would go out with the football players,
or "hunks" who never seemed to notice Beth, even though she had a "pretty
face."

Beth had dates, but never with the guys she admired or hoped would
admire her. She figured she would probably marry someday, but would have
to settle for what her mother termed "a decent guy with a nice smile." Beth
had no idea a real life *hunk* was in her future until she met Andy in her math
class during her last year of college. Andy thought Beth was a great girl,
highly intelligent, and had a fun personality. He valued these characteristics,
but wanted Beth to lose weight. He wanted her body to match her pretty face.
Andy pressured Beth to become thin like the models in Beth's favorite fashion magazines. Beth was in awe of Andy and promised to lose weight. She
tried all of the current diets and dietary supplements but did not achieve the
results both she and Andy wanted. Finally in a desperate measure, she opted
for gastric bypass surgery to help her lose weight and control her appetite.
She did not recuperate easily, nor did her weight *just fall off* as she and Andy
had hoped it would. Andy lost patience with the whole ordeal and distanced
himself from Beth. It is unfortunate Beth went through major surgery and
much anguish for the love of an elusive man with an eye for perfection.

Our Past Experiences with Family and Friends

We base some of our expectations about relationships from our past experiences. If we have had pleasant memories, we tend to be hopeful and outgoing. If our memories are painful, we tend to be careful and tentative. For
those who have been disappointed in love, it is understandable to anticipate
and worry that new love interests could potentially cause hurt as those who
have in the past.

Many of our couples have looked to the family and friends they admire for pointers on how to behave, what to do, and what to expect in certain romantic situations. Most people strive to be like those who we consider to "have it all together." We assume they know how to achieve the perfect balance based on our perception of their success in life.

It is human nature to generalize and put others in categories based on our past experiences. If someone looks like a person we know, we tend to attribute traits to him or her without getting to knowing them. We may expect them to act in a certain way just because they remind us of someone who looks like them. Of course this is the role of stereotyping that forms the roots of prejudice. Unfortunately, people often generalize about others based on little personal experience. Some people make a mistake and reject those who have the potential to be wonderful friends or future mates because they *think* they will not like this person.

As stated, we tend to adopt the opinions and attitudes of others we respect. We first pick up attitudes toward persons, places, and events from our family or guardians. We then turn to our teachers and friends for their input on what we should do and expect in certain situations. Right or wrong, they may offer advice based on their own personal experiences and biases.

Close friends and family members tend to influence what we come to expect in our relationships with others. They may tell how us to act on a first date, whether we should expect a call from a new friend, or if we should be the one who takes the initiative and makes the call. We develop expectations on when to allow that first kiss, how soon to meet a potential partner's parents, how much time to spend with a new love interest, how much money to spend on a birthday gift, what to expect for a holiday present after dating for a year, when it is okay to go on a vacation with a new love, and the frequency and intensity of intimate contact when one is dating or engaged.

We believe it is helpful to learn from our own mistakes and to listen to what others have to share. We can certainly learn from the mistakes and successes of others if the information we receive is not biased or presented with falsehoods. Ultimately we must decide what makes sense for us in our own lives, be it right or wrong. We learn from both our successes and our mistakes, so we must consider both types of experiences to be useful. Sometimes we become so traumatized by past hurts and disappointments that we stop learning. That happened to Cindy after falling in love with Tom.

Cindy was engaged to Tom for six months. Everything seemed to be progressing nicely. They were able to discuss and resolve disagreements about their wedding plans. Six weeks before the wedding, Tom told Cindy he met someone new and broke off their engagement. Cindy went into mourning for her lost love. She didn't date for a year despite protests from concerned family and friends. She finally agreed to go on selected blind dates but found herself very critical of everyone she met. If her dates expressed interest in pursuing a closer relationship, Cindy created impossible expectations her dates could not possibly attain. When these dates failed to please her, Cindy would become rejecting and push them away.

In therapy Cindy learned she was deeply afraid of being hurt. She realized she put up barriers that made it impossible for anyone to get close to her and hurt her as Tom did two years ago. Cindy learned to evaluate her expectations to determine which ones were realistic and those she needed to discard. In this process Cindy learned a new confidence in herself. Others observed this confidence and found her interesting and fun to be around. These positive experiences helped her to be open to experience love once again.

As our patients learn to set both individual and relationship goals that are readily attainable, they move closer to achieving their lifelong dreams together. By creating realistic expectations, they discover a vast improvement in their communication skills and levels of compatibility. This, in turn, improves their ability to trust, achieve closeness, and create intimacy with each other. This is a goal all of our couples share and enjoy in their romantic relationships. This is a goal we help our couples to fulfill in our relationship therapy sessions.

Chapter Ten

Flirting, Dating, and Intimacy

In chapter 5 we discussed compatibility and that certain spark one gets when in the presence of a love interest. As one becomes acquainted with a special person and feels that unique spark, he or she hopes the other person also feels the same intensity of attraction and interest toward them. So how does one send the message that they are interested in starting a relationship without scaring the other person away? We recommend good old fashioned fun and harmless flirting!

FUN FLIRTING

Being attracted to another person is both scary and exciting. It is scary because of the chance the other person will not feel the same way. It's scary to put one's heart on the line only to be rejected. Anyone who has ever been hurt can speak with authority on the pain they feel when told "no thank you" to a request for a date, or when they realize the good-looking guy in history class has been staring admirably at someone else.

I am sure many of us share high school memories of "getting up the courage" to say "Hi!" to that special person in the hallway. We can recall those heart-thumping, red-faced, sweaty-palmed feelings of youth. If we got a "Hi!" back, we quickly found our best friend to report the good news. If we failed to get a reasonable response, we were quick to report that too. Then we likely felt crushed for at least the rest of the day, if not longer.

Well those heart-thumping, red-faced, sweaty-palmed feelings are not confined to the young. They also pertain to the young at heart. They are present in all of us who feel that special scary excitement and desire when in the presence of a love interest. These are the feelings that tell us we have a crush, a real crush on someone new and interesting to us. These feelings are scary until we learn our fate: "Does he like me, or does he not?" "Will he reject me, or will he say 'Yes'"?

We recall with fondness the days of waking up in the morning with thoughts and fantasies of a new love interest. The excitement comes from the possibility that something wonderful may come of this crush. This person may be a future spouse; the love of one's life! The excitement comes from having a new adventure, a new goal, a new fantasy to share with special friends. The excitement comes from getting to know someone new, making a new friend, and making a fresh start with high hopes of having good luck in love.

So how do we let that special person know we are interested in them without looking foolish, or like a stalker? We definitely don't want to appear desperate, or scare them away! This question is best answered by *flirting*! Yes, good old fashioned flirting!

Some people are known as natural flirts. They may come across as flirts and not even know they are perceived as such. Their behavior is often considered charming. At the very least, they are considered approachable. The natural flirt likes to flirt just for fun. They are career flirts and do it quite often. They may flirt with many people in their everyday circle of acquaintances, but don't mean anything by it. When this person flirts, they are usually just being friendly, making conversation, or are manipulating you to do something for them. They may be seductive or they may be playful. They are charming and disarming. Nevertheless, they have skills most people can use to snare the interest of someone special.

Tips from a Career Flirt:

- *Smile:* This may sound simple, but we must be consciously aware of our facial expressions. When we smile at someone, we generally get a smile back, even from strangers. Smiling makes us appear friendly and approachable. Smiling makes us appear happy, both in general, and especially happy to see the person at whom we are smiling. Smiling can open up communication and makes the recipient feel positive and welcome to be in our presence. Smiling encourages others to approach for conversation around the canapés. Smiling encourages others to flirt back. So go ahead and smile. It's free, and it feels good!
- *Make eye contact:* When we are in the presence of a love interest, it is common to feel shy and embarrassed. We are concerned they will know our feelings and will not return them. We are concerned they know how we feel even though we have not uttered a word. These shy and embarrassed feelings may cause us to look away from a love interest. Yet, when we look away, we may appear aloof, preoccupied, disinterested, or per-

haps interested in someone else who is in our field of vision. So as difficult as it may seem, it is important to make direct eye contact when flirting with a love interest. This allows the person to feel he or she is the sole focus of our attention. Once eye contact is made, it is important to *smile!* Remember, being the sole focus of someone's attention is indeed a compliment!

- *Use the person's name:* When speaking to a love interest, remember to use his or her name when involved in a conversation, however brief the interaction. Most of us consider it a compliment when a person has gone to the trouble of learning and remembering our name. It helps to personalize the interaction. It tells the recipient you know who they are and they are at least an acquaintance of yours. So when greeting a love interest, say "Hi George," or "Hi Emily." When introducing a love interest to a friend, use their name as well.

- *Touching:* The act of touching someone new in your life can be tricky. Career flirts touch often, but are not necessarily intending to be seductive. It is important to note that touching when flirting is not meant to seduce the love interest, unless the relationship has advanced to an intimate level. Rather, it is a way to communicate and express interest. Touching may include putting a hand on a shoulder or arm for a brief moment. It may include a quick pat on a hand when sitting and talking on a park bench. It may be a hand on the mid to lower back when crossing the street. The touch that is best used is light and does not linger beyond a few seconds. The flirt does not touch any private part of the body that may indicate sexual desire unless involved in a romantic relationship with this person and knows they have permission to touch in this way. A hand that lingers may be unwanted by the recipient. It may be considered too forward. A hand that lingers may be considered a seductive gesture. Seductive gestures include a touch with one or two fingers in the inside of an arm or leg, face, head, on the breasts or genitalia, or on the neck, stomach, or buttocks. These gestures are best reserved for a romantic relationship in which both persons have consented to touch and be touched in this way.

- *Sit close:* We suggest you decrease the physical distance between yourself and your love interest, but avoid crowding this person or invading his or her space. It is important to respect the need for adequate physical distance when speaking to someone. Yet we have noticed that career flirts reduce this distance just a bit. They may move in closer when seated on a couch or when in conversation with someone. Sitting close or leaning in to someone lets them know you are interested in the interaction you are having with them. It lets a person know you find them interesting and enjoyable to be with perhaps more than anyone else in the room. It creates a sense of closeness or even intimacy without being intimate with them. It signals to the rest of the people in the room that your conversation is private.

- *Copy body positions:* Social scientists have observed that couples or individuals who are having a positive social interaction will mirror each other's body language. If a person has his legs crossed, the other person involved in the conversation will often do the same. This simple gesture seems to increase familiarity and is a less obvious way to flirt.

- *Give a compliment:* While smiling, say something simple such as "I like that shirt" or "Is that dress new?" A similar comment shows interest and allows the recipient to feel noticed and therefore good about himself. Everyone loves to be complimented, especially if the compliment is genuine and does not come across as phony or forced. Compliments do not always have to pertain to the person's appearance. A compliment can relate to what the person has recently achieved, such as offering congratulations on a new promotion, a presentation done well, or even a sharp new car.

- *Be considerate:* If you see your love interest has his hands full, be sure to ask if you can carry something to ease his load. Ask him if he wants something to eat or drink when at a party. Be polite and say "thank you" when the situation is appropriate. Extend concern or condolences if you have learned he has had misfortune or has suffered a loss in his life. This will show the love interest you have genuine care and concern for him. Good manners definitely go a long way when flirting with a love interest.

- *Be attractive:* When you know you may see your love interest, be sure to be clean, neat, and wear clothing that enhances your physical assets. Make sure the outfit you are wearing is coordinated. It's a good idea to match slacks and socks, blouses and skirts. The appropriate use of cologne, makeup, and jewelry can increase a person's attractiveness to others as well. Of utmost importance is good personal hygiene. Freshly brushed teeth, combed hair, clothing free of stains or hanging threads speak volumes. Body odor, bad breath, greasy hair, and soiled clothing speaks volumes as well, and may lead to quick rejection.

- *Suggest something fun to do:* It is important to learn what your love interest enjoys doing. Inquire about their favorite hobbies and leisure activities. When the moment is right, take a risk and ask the new love interest to go somewhere or do something you would both enjoy. This is your first date, and it may be the beginning of something new and wonderful.

MEGA-FLIRTING

We previously discussed flirting with a prospective mate earlier in this chapter. We now want to up the ante, so to speak, and suggest flirtatious measures that are more bold and to the point. Here are some tips:

- Send a suggestive message to your prospective lover or spouse. The message could read, *meet you at seven, can't wait to touch you, be close to you*, and so forth. I think you get the idea. Send or hand deliver flowers with a teddy bear and a provocative message idea!
- Play spa, and give your loved one a facial, massage, or a manicure. Allow these simple pleasures to get hotter with kissing and more.
- Take bubble baths together. Let your fingers do the talking under the bubbles.
- Shop together for new bedclothes and then wear them that evening.
- Smile, make eye contact with your mate, and then rub your fingers through his hair.
- Wear something your lover considers sexy.
- Perform grooming rituals in front of your mate. These may include dressing or undressing, shaving, putting on lipstick, or spraying perfume on the back of your knee.
- Light a candle, and play soft music while you compliment your mate's body.
- Read a book on sex acts and practice what you read.
- Watch a provocative video and enjoy a little romp of your own.

FINDING SOMEONE TO DATE

When you have decided you want to start dating, you have a decision to make: where to find potential partners. This is not as easy as it seems. The answer depends on your philosophy of dating and what methods are comfortable for you. Check the following list for some ideas, and add some items of your own. We believe it is important to know all the alternatives so you can decide the best venue for yourself.

- *School:* In this atmosphere, you can get to know your love interest before dating him. You can observe him around others and determine if he has the characteristics you are seeking. This can be in a university setting, adult education classes, taking golf lessons, or going to dog training classes. It is a great idea to take classes in a favorite hobby or passion. The budding photographer may meet many classmates who share his interest.

- *Work:* Some companies and organizations frown on fraternization at work. The concern is the romantic relationship may cause a distraction for those involved and for others who are curious about the relationship. Idle gossip among co-workers may interfere with productivity and may create a negative work environment. Also, if the relationship does not work out, there may be negative interactions between the couple that may take place at work. Of course we can all understand the issues dating would create in a professional environment. Nevertheless, we think the work place is potentially a great location to observe others and meet a potential mate. It is important to keep in mind that these relationships are best kept a secret from co-workers until or unless the relationship becomes serious and a marriage is being scheduled.
- *Clubs or Organizations:* Here you will meet someone who likely shares at least one interest with you and is the interested in the activities offered by the club. You may find others interesting in making objects out of stained glass or writing newspaper articles. It is also fun to join local civic or political organizations to support your causes and meet new friends. Similar to school and work, you can spend time with your love interest and enjoy a common goal or philosophy before asking the person out for a date.
- *Religious Institutions:* Going to services is another good way to meet and observe a prospective partner. In a religious institution, you may meet others who share your religious beliefs, customs, and background. You may also have the advantage of observing and possibly meeting his or her family before going on your first date. Some religious institutions sponsor singles events that are another good venue for meeting new friends.
- *Cultural Events:* Buy season tickets to the opera or the local concert hall or theater group. There may be other singles you can chat with during intermission. Go to museums, the zoo, and free concerts in the park. Check to see if museums in your town have singles events. These may include lectures and receptions just for you.
- *Walk Your Dog:* Go to dog parks, dog shows, or any dog event where you can show off your best friend. Join a dog training class or breed club. A stroll around town may be the perfect venue to find other single animal lovers.
- *Singles Cruises:* There are vacation destinations especially for singles. Check with your travel agent for some fun places to meet and greet others.
- *Shopping:* Singles often like to shop. It's an inexpensive way to be around lots of people. It's a way to get out of the house on a rainy Saturday afternoon if you are stuck at home alone with nothing to do. It is possible to meet a new friend while picking out a new sweater for your brother. Check out the local supermarkets as well. Some are offering singles nights.

- *Blind Dates/Set-Ups:* Consider allowing your mother, brother, or best friend to set you up. It's only for one night and you may meet someone terrific. Be sure to meet this new person in your life in a public setting such as a restaurant, coffee bar, or theater. It is not safe in today's world to invite strangers to your home.
- *Parties:* If you are invited, by all means go. Okay, you may be tired from a long work week, tired of disappointing relationships, or just plain bored. But go to the party anyway. You may have a good time in spite of feeling down on the whole dating scene. Check with the host or hostess to see if there are any singles attending. If not, you may want to attend anyway to meet other couples who may know of a terrific single person looking for love.
- *"In Search Of" Ads:* You can place an ad for a love interest in a local publication. It's okay to brag a bit about all of your assets. Be upfront about those you are seeking in a potential date. Be honest about your age, height, and weight. Be sure to meet at a public place for a bite to eat or a cup of tea or coffee. We again urge that invitations to your home are postponed until you have had a few dates and feel comfortable and safe with this new person in your life.
- *Professional Match Making Services:* You can sign up with an agency who will charge you a fee for matching your interests and attributes with others they have in their data bank. You may fill out a questionnaire, provide photos, or make a video of yourself in which you will describe your likes and dislikes, and what you are looking for in a mate. Be sure to check out this service before paying a fee and signing on the dotted line. You will want to ascertain the service is a legitimate business.
- *Internet Dating Services:* Some of these services are free, others charge a fee. There are services for individuals of all ages. As stated above, do your homework and check out all dating services, especially on the internet, before signing on the dotted line.

HOW TO DATE GREAT

Once you have found someone to date, try to have fun in all of your activities. Whether you date for a short period of time, become engaged, or marry, it is important to be open and willing to experience new and exciting adventures. We encourage our couples to do things they have never done before to widen their skills and interests. We also suggest they participate in activities that may bore them but will bring joy to their date.

Here are other ways to be a great date, from the first date straight through to your fiftieth wedding anniversary and beyond.

- Throughout your relationship, show empathy, respect, and regard for your date's feelings. Listen closely and show genuine concern for his fears and joys.
- Avoid "talking over" your mate because you are in a hurry for her to finish her story. Wait for her to finish her story before cutting in to add your comments or questions.
- Avoid being critical. Instead be a positive problem solver. Help fix the leaking sink or find a good plumber rather than complain the faucet is dripping. Clean the house together, rather than complain that it is dirty. Remember no one is perfect, and the best way to help a boyfriend to develop more positive behaviors is to both demonstrate them yourself and give constructive advice on how to improve the behavior in question.
- Occasionally surprise your lover with little tokens of affection. An "I love you" note in a lunch bag, a note card that expresses a warm thought, a single rose, his favorite crackers from the supermarket, or any other item you know he would cherish because it came from you.
- Do your fair share of household responsibilities without being nagged or told it is your turn to do the dishes or feed the dog. Taking initiative is considered an important trait in a respectful and cooperative spouse.
- Take time out from a busy schedule to spend quality time with your mate. Plan regularly scheduled dates and don't cancel them unless there is a true emergency! You both need to take time to review the events of the day; do so on a daily basis. Remember to try to have dinner together on a daily basis. This is a good time to catch up on family news.
- Be supportive when life presents challenges. When the going gets tough, a spouse needs his partner most of all. Make yourself available to hear about the problems that are worrying your spouse. Don't be in a hurry! Listen attentively and make constructive suggestions on how the challenges can be solved rather than criticize him for having the problem. Happy couples tell us their spouses are their best friends. So when the going gets tough, confide in your best friend so he knows what is happening in your life. If you keep important information to yourself, you and your spouse may likely drift apart.
- Be patient with your mate. Not everyone understands or does activities, chores, or figures out glitches with the computer at the same speed. We all have our strengths and weaknesses. Help your spouse build on her strengths while bolstering her weaknesses. Remember no one is perfect or even smart, sexy, sophisticated, capable, or funny all of the time.
- Ask what she wants for her birthday, anniversary, or special occasion. Then consider her wishes before making your purchase. Some spouses would rather not be surprised at gift-giving time. Instead, they prefer to get a gift they truly want. We have found many spouses consider gift giving a mirror of the relationship. Considerate or good gift givers are

considered to be more in love with their spouse, and more in touch with her tastes, needs, and desires. So when out shopping, observe your spouse making second and third glances at certain favored items. Then be sure to add these items to your gift ideas list.

- Respect a mate's need for alone time or time needed to recover from a long day at work. We tell everyone that at least thirty minutes is required to recover from a day's work. A way to recover is to take a shower, go for a walk, play a game on the computer, or take a nap. It is difficult to tolerate a discussion of life's problems, what appliances are broken, or the bills that arrived in the mail when one enters the door at 6 p.m. In the same vein, everyone needs time for his or herself. Happy couples tell us their spouses are considerate of one another when a request is made for a day to go fishing, shopping, enjoying time with friends, and so forth. Of course if a spouse takes advantage of this generosity, then conflicts in the relationship will likely occur. It's important to consider a balance in this issue. A balance occurs when each spouse is granted a similar amount of alone time to enjoy.
- Do everyday activities together. Buy items for a delicious meal, cook the food side by side, eat by candlelight, and then clean up together. Chores are more fun when shared. Chores take less time when done together. Many of our happy couples believe it is *romantic* to do chores or run errands together.
- Be affectionate in private and in public. Touching is important for marital and emotional health. A peck on the cheek and a pat on the arm are comforting and supportive gestures. Sit close at parties; make eye contact when speaking. Show the world you are indeed a couple, but leave intimate or sexual behaviors for private moments.
- Be loyal. No affairs, no sexting, no chat rooms, no nothing! Happy couples treat each other with respect. They honor their commitment to each other. They respect the vows they have spoken to each other. They respect themselves for having the integrity to stay true to their spouse. They have healthy boundaries with others with whom they interact. They do not engage in flirting with others. They discourage others from flirting with them. They do not try to get affection, attention, or validation from others if they believe it is lacking in their relationship with their spouse. Instead, they discuss their feelings with their spouse, use effective and positive problem-solving skills, and seek advice from professionals who are highly trained and experienced in advising those who have relationship problems.
- Pace yourself. Savor the relationship and don't rush it. Too often new relationships begin with a flurry of ten texts a day; four-hour telephone conversations; frequent dates, even on work or school nights; rushed intimacy, and statements of love and promises of the future together. It is truly rare for a rushed relationship to endure. These relationships burn out

all too frequently. No one can truly maintain such a frantic pace. It is important to not set a pace that cannot be continued as the relationship matures. It is equally important to understand that a slowing of this initial flurry of activity in a new relationship is not necessarily a sign that the relationship is ending. Instead it may be the beginning of a new phase of comfort and trust that a relationship can endure without constant contact with one another. Remember the tortoise truly did beat the hare by a slow and steady pace.

A Fun Date, A Great Mate

Henry was indeed a great date. His wife Marge considered herself very lucky. Henry was an interesting person. He often took courses or went to lectures to enhance his knowledge in a variety of subjects. He enjoyed sharing the information he learned with Marge. He always suggested doing new things and going to interesting places on their weekly dates. Henry and Marge collected souvenirs from their many outings. They referred to their souvenirs often as they reflected on the fun times they had together. Henry was also very interested in looking and feeling his best. He exercised regularly, ate healthy foods, and was always clean and well dressed. Despite the fact that he had a demanding and stressful job, he never brought his frustrations from work home with him. Henry was always there for Marge. The night she lost her mother was especially difficult for her. Henry was there to comfort her. He always set aside time for them to just talk about their experiences, thoughts, and feelings. As much as he enjoyed being in Marge's company, he always respected her need to spend time by herself or with friends and family members. As Marge always said, she was a "lucky mate who was married to a great date."

Henry has all of the attributes of a great date and a great spouse. He is supportive, considerate, loving, warm, loyal, and most of all in love with his wife. There are many men like Henry in the world looking for their version of Marge to spend their lives with.

Date Nights

We encourage our couples (dating, engaged, and married) to try to date one night a week. The spouses can take turns planning their weekly dates. The person who is planning the date tries to think of an activity that will especially interest his partner. Examples include playing board games, renting a video, planning a pizza and popcorn evening, taking a walk, or going out to eat. Dates need not be long, expensive, or formal. They are designed to make an enjoyable evening for both involved in the date. By planning a date, the spouse shows thoughtfulness, consideration, and a willingness to please her mate. During date nights, it is essential to avoid discussion of problem areas. Date nights are best scheduled when there are few if any distractions and annoyances present. Date nights are the time to hire a baby sitter, shut off the cell phones, and tell your family and friends you are too busy to talk to them at that moment. Date nights can involve romantic gestures such as holding hands, kissing, tender caresses, sexual relations, or nothing at all. There are no rules. The idea is to create a pleasant evening for both of you. If your spouse has a miserable cold on date night, then serve hot chicken soup, or get take-out Chinese food. Then cuddle up under a warm and cozy blanket and take a nap together. Date night is as simple as that! After each date, be sure to open your *Date Night Log* and document what activities you chose for your date. Then both of you will sign and date the entry. See chapter 11 for details.

THE NOT SO GREAT DATE

Peg was married to Vinny. She was a very insecure person since she was a little girl. Her mother died when she was very young. Her father dated one woman after another and was quite unstable after Peg's mother died. Peg went to live with her uncle's family. She never felt like she belonged with them. She needed lots of reassurance that they wanted her, but that was not forthcoming. She followed her aunt and uncle around the house looking for some sign that she belonged in their family. Peg married Vinny right out of high school. Despite the fun they had together, her insecurity didn't fade. She was possessive of his time and rarely allowed him to get together with family and friends without insisting she be included. When Vinny went out, she occasionally spied on him to determine if he was cheating on her. In an effort to control Vinny, Peg often said she was "sick" to manipulate him to stay home. Once or twice she even expected him to stay home from work so she could make sure he wasn't "having fun conversing with co-workers." When Vinny confronted her annoying and clinging ways, Peg became defensive and accused him of lying and cheating. Then Peg withdrew to their bedroom where she waited for Vinny to come and apologize to her.

Vinny was tired of Peg's behavior and pursued marital therapy. Peg went to individual sessions as well. She gained insight into her challenging behaviors, and ultimately encouraged Vinny to attend night school to finish his college degree. She promised Vinny that when he finished, she was next!

Our therapy with these couples involves exploring their history of intimacy, both together and with others in their past. We discuss if other problems exist in their relationship that are impacting on their current sexual interactions. We may suggest both marital and individual therapy to address those problems. Depending on the presenting issues and perceived causes, we make suggestions for future treatment so sexual pleasures are again a healthy part of their lives.

All of these gestures can keep a relationship young and fresh. Be sure to spend time with each other when you are both relaxed. Keep the conversation light. Try not to discuss issues that concern you before you intend to be intimate. When the moment approaches and the romantic fires begin to smolder, allow the intensity of your feelings for one another to ignite.

INTIMACY

Intimacy can be described in many ways. It can be expressed as flirting, having a heart-to-heart talk, making eye contact, or simply by touching in a gentle, yet provocative manner. It can involve many forms of sexual contact. In today's world, it can also be defined as sexting, which includes sex related or sexually provocative conversations via text. Many of our patients have reported that pressures from today's world have negatively impacted the degree to which they spend quality time together. Much time is spent attending to mounting stressors from work, children, and finances, ill parents, and so forth. The result is that many couples are too tired to enjoy sexual pleasures with each other. They feel this aspect of their relationship has become more awkward, less familiar, and even estranged. They may feel less comfortable making sexual overtures toward their spouse for fear of rejection. Many of our couples state their relationship is fine except that they rarely share intimate moments, and they miss the warm contact they once shared earlier in their relationship when their lives were less stressful and busy. The following are some "do's" and "don'ts" for your intimate moments:

Do:

- Go slow and allow your passion for each other to build. If time is an issue, postpone your date for another day.
- Allow yourself time to get in the mood. Wear something sexy. Do whatever it takes to feel attractive and alluring. Wear a pleasant scent, brush your teeth, make sure your body and clothes are clean and fresh. Then set the mood by creating an ambiance that encourages love and affection.
- Intimacy is a sensual and a sexual process. Use your five senses to help you enjoy your spouse. Touch and kiss your mate's face, cuddle close, lightly squeeze a thigh, lick an ear lobe, enjoy the scent of cologne or massage oil, and watch your spouse smile with pleasure.

- Compliment your spouse on his adorable dimple and then kiss it. Admire her body with soft sensual kisses. Give your mate positive feedback as you explore each others' bodies. Smile often and make cooing noises to show you are pleased with the affection you are receiving.
- Communicate your needs by gently gliding your spouse's hand to where you want to be touched. Kindly let her know where to put more pressure. Indicate your pleasure at being touched in the right location.
- Share in the enjoyment of the moment. Allow your mate sufficient time to achieve satisfaction. Orgasm is not done on a schedule, nor is it a race to see who gets there first. When or if orgasm is not reached, allow your spouse to relax and enjoy cuddling before ending the lovemaking session. Offer reassurance rather than criticism when your spouse's performance is a bit off. Avoid expressing blame or displeasure at this time. Tomorrow is another day!
- Remove the pressure to be close when your spouse is tired, stressed, is not in the mood, or does not feel well. Select evenings when just cuddling is sufficient. Some of the most romantic moments are spent lying peacefully in each other's arms.
- Be adventurous by trying new positions and techniques. Plan a trip to an adult store to stock up on fun sex toys and aides to keep your relationship new and hot. Experiment with different massage oils to prolong the evening. Make love in different locations in the house.
- Be respectful by asking your mate if she prefers sex in the morning, afternoon, or evening. Everyone has their favorite time of day when fires of passion are at their peak.
- Always be neat and clean. Closeness requires good personal hygiene. Make sure your bed linens are clean as well. No cracker crumbs and dirty tissues allowed.
- After being close, linger for a while and just cuddle or take a nap together.

Don't:

- Assume your mate is in the mood when you are and force your intensions on her. This is called *rape* and is considered a crime, married or not. Check out her desires and needs before making sexy moves toward her. If she is not in the mood for intimacy, save your moves for another day when she may be more receptive.
- Approach your mate after you have been working in the yard for the past three hours, or have not brushed your teeth recently. Body and breath odor are turn-offs. It does not take long to shave, shower, and brush your teeth. Make sure you take the time to do all of the above.

- Make a mad dash for the door after being intimate. No one wants to feel they are being used just for sex or that the lovemaking session was so bad you can't wait to get out of town.
- Make or receive phone calls, emails, or texts while being close. In any language or culture that is considered rude behavior.
- Criticize your spouse for not performing at her best or for not being in the mood for sex. Instead, ask him what he wants to do at that time and respect those wishes and preferences.
- Force or manipulate your date to do something she does not want to do or criticize her for having her own preferences. Not everyone likes oral sex or trying certain sexual positions. Give your date encouragement to try new things. In time he may gradually open up to the adventures you suggest.
- Criticize your boyfriend's body. Instead, encourage him to lose weight or firm up by exercising together. Compliment those aspects of your date that you love the best. Maybe it is his smile, her hair, or his eyes that you can admire during lovemaking.
- Discuss your problems at work when in bed. Discussion of problems of any sort is sure to destroy the mood you are trying so hard to establish.
- State you are turned on by another person and then expect your lover to want to be close to you. Now is not the time to say your new secretary has a hot body or that your former girlfriend was a more energetic lover.
- Watch television or a movie while your mate is trying to entice you. Avoid distractions of any kind so you can enjoy each other's company to the fullest.
- Forget an important occasion such as your anniversary or your mate's birthday and expect closeness that day. It's likely not going to happen!
- Have sex just to get pregnant rather than for the sheer joy of being close. That creates a lot of pressure for both of you.

There may be times when a spouse is not in the mood for love making. It's important to keep pressure out of the bedroom. Intimacy is more than intercourse. Holding hands or sharing a glass of bubbly can arouse closeness as well. Coaxing a spouse to be close or using guilt to force the issue are definite mood busters.

When a spouse is unable to be in the mood for intimacy for an extended period of time, it may be helpful to rule out a medical or psychological condition that may be contributing to this situation.

NOT IN THE MOOD FOR LOVE

There may be various reasons why the mood for love eludes us. Here is a sample of those reasons:

- *Depression*: Chronic sadness can deplete energy for most tasks, including lovemaking. It's important to see a professional if feelings of sadness extend over weeks to months. There may be a chemical imbalance causing these symptoms, or a need for psychotherapy and/or medication to treat the chronic sadness.
- *Drugs and alcohol*: Use or abuse of drugs or alcohol can cause fatigue and dull one's senses. The use of substances can cause one to misperceive or misinterpret not only the behavior of a spouse, but one's own behavior as well. It is best to "sleep off" the effects of those substances that have a negative effect on one's judgment and perceptions of reality.
- *Stress*: This is the greatest energy zapper and mood deflator. Stress can cause one to be in an irritable mood. It lowers frustration tolerance and can cause one to overreact to events or actions of others.
- *Physical illness*: Even minor physical upsets such as a nasty cold or diarrhea can take away your mood for amour. Vaginitis can be painful and cause a woman to avoid intercourse. More serious illnesses where an individual feels very ill can affect an amorous mood. Ailments such as arthritis can cause a mood to sour due to being uncomfortable in certain prone positions.
- *Hormonal changes and imbalances*: As women age, their hormone levels change and there is less testosterone. This can affect a desire for sex as well as physical discomfort due to the thinning of the vaginal walls. Prescribed medical treatment is available for hormonal issues.
- *Erectile dysfunction*: This is a bothersome ailment that interferes with performance and self-esteem. Again, a male with this issue is encouraged to consult with a physician to determine the correct course of action. At times erectile dysfunction is due to emotional and/or physical issues. Nevertheless, it is best to be evaluated by a professional so the symptoms can be treated.
- *General anxiety*: Any condition that causes concern about performance or being close to another individual can interfere with a longing for intimacy. Anxiety can cause erectile dysfunction and other performance related issues. Again, a professional consultation is suggested so these symptoms can be alleviated.

- *Anger:* Being angry at a partner can interfere with a desire to be close. It is best to postpone intimacy when one or both parties are in an angry mood. The best advice is to talk about the reasons for the anger to see if a solution or compromise is available. Once the anger is resolved, then attempts at intimacy can take place.
- *Medications:* There are prescription medications that can affect sexual performance and male potency. It is important to talk to a physician regarding the side effects of certain prescribed drugs.

As stated, a physician and/or a therapist should be consulted to treat these symptoms. Too often a partner is embarrassed and does not wish to consult a physician. This happened to Joan and Perry.

Joan and Perry married when they were in their early forties. Joan wanted to start a family immediately since she feared she had little time left to conceive a baby, especially since her mother began menopause at an early age. Perry consented, but he knew he had a problem with erectile dysfunction. He failed to discuss this issue with Joan. He blamed his dysfunction on the long hours he spent at work. Joan suggested they go on vacation as a *cure* for this problem. Perry consented but insisted on bringing paper work with him that he "had to get done." Perry felt much pressure to perform so they could conceive a baby. He started to spend more time at the office, and often came home after Joan had already gone to bed. On weekends, he spent much time in their home office. He began to distance himself from Joan more and more. They did not go out on dates, nor spend time relaxing in their newly furnished family room. Joan found other things to do to occupy her time, but continued to long for a child. She suggested that she and Perry have date nights, but he did not have time for fun. Feeling desperate, Joan suggested they try artificial insemination by using Perry's sperm, but he refused, stating it was "unnatural." Eventually Joan's longing for a child caused her to leave Perry. Within a year, she met someone new and found out she was pregnant. Perry started to spend fewer hours at the office. He no longer needed to avoid Joan or her demands to have intercourse. He eventually spoke to his doctor about his problem and started therapy where he discussed his performance anxiety issues. He was eventually free from this disorder and secretly wished he had gone to therapy sooner and discussed his problem with Joan so they could be together. It was too late for a future with Joan but not too late to find a new love, which Perry eventually did!

We always suggest that our couples talk to their physicians about emotional and physical issues that effect lovemaking. It is important to rule out an underlying medical problem. Once a medical problem is either ruled out or treated, then we can discuss the possibility of psychological and relationship reasons for the presenting problem.

Throughout therapy we remind our couples to continue to flirt, date, and discuss their fears, concerns, fantasies, and desires regarding their relationship and needs for intimacy. This is important to achieve a happy and healthy relationship. We wish that for you as well!

BREAKING UP IS HARD FOR SOME AND EASY FOR OTHERS

So many of my patients come in to describe their break-ups with those they dated. More often than not their break-ups occur without any type of closure. What happens is one person seems to *fade away* from the other. There are fewer texts, shorter telephone conversations, lack of interest in their girlfriend or boyfriend's life, and vagueness about putting future dates on the calendar. This lack of closure regarding what went wrong in the relationship creates much anxiety for the person on the receiving end of the "break-up." So what is a person to do? Most often, the one who is left behind searches through his or her memory of the dates and conversations that took place during the relationship. Text messages are read and reread in search of clues that might indicate why the relationship that held so much promise is now on the wane or has ended. Since they do not know why they were left behind, most individuals essentially "fill in the blanks" by coming up with excusable reasons for the behavior that left them struggling with self-doubt and feelings of inadequacy. The filled in blanks may include "he has been really busy at work," "her mother is drinking again," "he has been really tired," "she hasn't changed our status on Facebook, so I guess we are still together," "he needs to spend more time with his daughter," and so forth. All this exhausting mental work is done in an effort to pinpoint what the deal breaker was, and to see if they were to blame for the sadness they feel.

So now we face the inevitable question, what do you do? Do you confront the person about why he or she is not interested in dating anymore? Do you risk being told you were not pretty enough, smart enough, rich enough, successful enough? Do you risk further evasive behavior and not being told anything but a vague excuse about work, timing, stress, or a stubbed big toe? Do you search for an answer or just let it go? This is a tough question to answer, for there are no hard-and-fast rules. The answer really depends on the degree of openness and willingness for both parties to be honest and explore reasons for the break-up. It depends on the maturity of the person who left the relationship and whether he or she can effectively cope with confrontation. It depends on whether the person who left the relationship truly understands his or her feelings and can explain them to someone about whom they may still have feelings of care and concern. It is obvious the decision to confront or not confront depends on many factors. It is important to know why the break-up occurred if only not to repeat the same dating blunders in their next relationship. It is important to learn how to accept a break-up and then let it go graciously and respectfully without trying to talk the person out of his or her decision, or making the person feel much blame or foolishness.

Breaking Up with Finesse

My belief is if you are mature enough to enter into a relationship, you have the responsibility to end the relationship with an honest explanation of what went wrong. This needs to be done with finesse. That requires consideration of the other person's feelings. Constructive criticism is fine, but character assassination is not. There is no need to tell the other person she is too fat, a sloppy kisser, does not live in a nice house, and so forth. What you can say is you do not see a future with this person, you do not have enough in common to go on dating, you do not have enough passion for this person, or you have an interest to date others. There are many considerate ways to end a relationship, but there must be closure! The relationship must have a definite beginning and a definite end.

When a patient comes in and tearfully discusses a break-up, it is important to help them understand they can live through this painful time of their life. They will not shatter; rather they will endure the pain they feel. They are asked to not assume they were not good enough for the other person, and that this was their last chance at love and no one will ever want them. They are asked to confront their mistakes, learn from them, and promise themselves they will not repeat them. They are encouraged to seek the company and support from significant others in their lives, to say "yes" to invitations to attend social events and "yes" to opportunities to date and take a chance at love once again.

Chapter Eleven

Creating a Resource Library

In our marital and relationship therapy model, we suggest that our patients develop a resource library that is specially designed for their specific needs and issues. No two patient libraries are ever the same. We suggest that our patients create the following notebooks: *Needs Notebook, Conflict Resolution Notebook, Date Night Log, Relationship Memories Book, and a Family Meeting Book.*

NEEDS NOTEBOOK

The *Needs Notebook* is a tool to help the couple avoid miscommunication and confusion about what each other needs and wants from one another. It takes away the need for mind reading and serves as a vehicle that allows the couple to communicate their needs to each other. It also serves as a guide that allows the couple's needs to be addressed accurately and in a timely manner. We have learned that a couple can be married for many decades and still not know what each other truly needs. One cannot make the assumption that longevity in a relationship guarantees this knowledge. The *Needs Notebook* will never be completed during the life of the relationship. There will always be needs that will be added by the couple. Further, it will serve as a useful resource that enhances their relationship. It is for the couple to learn from and enjoy.

The *Needs Notebook* is a tool to help the couple avoid miscommunication and confusion about what each other needs and wants from one another. It takes away the need for mind reading and serves as a vehicle that allows the couple to communicate their needs to each other. It also serves as a guide that allows the couple's needs to be addressed accurately and in a timely manner.

We have learned that a couple can be married for many decades and still not know what each other truly needs. One cannot make the assumption that longevity in a relationship guarantees this knowledge. The *Needs Notebook* will never be completed during the life of the relationship. There will always be needs that will be added by the couple. Further, it will serve as a useful resource that enhances their relationship. It is for the couple to learn from and enjoy.

The couple creates their own *Needs Notebook* together. It identifies needs they would like to address with each other. There are often needs common to every couple, such as *when I am happy, I need*. There are also needs specific to a couple, such as *when I come home from a business trip, I need.*

To be most effective, the couple decides which needs to address in a specific order. We help our couples start to define their needs by giving them a *Needs Questionnaire* to complete individually. Then we review their answers in our sessions. Some of our couples have stated they prefer to respond to the questionnaire by changing the word *need* to *want*. We follow each need statement with what the spouse does not need in that given topic area. The needs that are addressed are on the *Needs Questionnaire* form that is presented in this chapter. Contents from the *Needs Questionnaire* and other general or specific needs that each spouse identifies comprise what we refer to as the *Needs Notebook* . As we review the *Needs Questionnaire* in therapy, we ask each spouse to write his or her own needs on this form with no input from their partner. The couple may agree to work on five needs per week and then exchange their questionnaires for review.

It is important that each spouse address the same need at the same time, so they can systematically progress through the list of needs. For instance, in the specific example above about the business trip, only one spouse may actually travel for business. In that case, the traveler would address, *When I return from a business trip, I need*, and the non-traveler would add, *When you return from a business trip, I need.* Once the *Needs Questionnaire* is reviewed entirely in therapy, we can then discuss other needs the couple has identified that are not on the *Needs Questionnaire* but are in their customized *Needs Notebook.*

Needs Questionnaire

> When I am happy, I need . . .
> I don't need . . .
>
> When I am sad, I need . . .
> I don't need . . .
>
> On my birthday, I need . . .
> I don't need . . .

After a bad day at home, work, or school, I need . . .
　　I don't need . . .

When I am sick, I need . . .
　　I don't need . . .

When I am under stress, I need . . .
　　I don't need . . .

When I want to celebrate a success or good news, I need . . .
　　I don't need . . .

On holidays or on special events, I need . . .
　　I don't need . . .

When I desire physical intimacy, I need . . .
　　I don't need . . .

When I need to solve a personal or work related problem, I need . . .
　　I don't need . . .

When I am angry I need . . .
　　I don't need . . .

When there are chores to be done, I need . . .
　　I don't need . . .

When I am scared or nervous about something, I need . . .
　　I don't need . . .

When I want support, I need . . .
　　I don't need . . .

When I could use a "time out," I need . . .
　　I don't need . . .

When I want to discuss something important, I need . . .
　　I don't need . . .

The *Needs Notebook* is a valuable tool that serves many functions, such as the following:

The Needs Notebook Takes the "Shoulds" Out of the Relationship

We have heard many spouses make statements such as "We have been married for ten years; my husband *should* know what I want for my birthday." The problem is that none of us are mind readers. We assume our spouse knows our needs and wants so we don't have to speak our minds. The fact remains that to avoid disappointment, everyone—married or single—must say what they want or need in any given situation. By using the *Needs*

Notebook, we have the opportunity to gain this knowledge and avoid making mistakes in the future. By using the *Needs Notebook*, a wife can state exactly what she wants her mate to do when they are having a party. A husband can state what he likes to eat on his birthday.

The Needs Notebook Takes the Guesswork Out of a Relationship

Many of our spouses have stated they think they know how their mate will react or what their mate will need in a certain situation. They tend to *second guess* this information. Unfortunately, many husbands and wives do not really know their spouse well enough to make a correct assumption. For example, "I think my husband will like this couch for his office. I'll buy it for him." Or, "Oh, I guess my wife will want to go to the party. I'll accept the invitation for both of us." By using a *Needs Notebook*, the wife will learn that her husband would prefer to pick out his own furniture for his office. The husband will find out that his wife does not like her husband to accept invitations without consulting her first.

By reading these examples, you can see how referring to a *Needs Notebook* can prevent many disagreements, disappointments, and quarrels in a relationship.

The Needs Notebook Is Never Ending

No one is expected to know what he or she will need or want in every situation for the remainder of our lives. The *Needs Notebook* is an ever-evolving text. It is never finished because as we live our lives, we tend to discover more personal and general needs that must be addressed. There will always be additional entries that relate to new feelings and situations that may arise for each spouse.

The Needs Notebook as a Useful Resource

We do not expect each person to memorize his or her spouse's *Needs Notebook*. We do expect our couples refer to their *Needs Notebook* on a frequent basis so they can always be aware of their mate's needs across various situations. We suggest that the *Needs Notebook* be kept in a central location so it is never lost or misplaced. On a bookshelf in the family room or on a night stand in the bedroom are good locations to consider.

The Needs Notebook Enhances Self Knowledge

We must be aware of our own needs before we can realistically expect that another person, even our spouse can know this information. I have spoken to many patients who are completely unaware of what they need in life. The general concept of *needs* seems to be elusive. It appears that many individuals go through their lives in an almost robotic fashion. They get up in the morning and automatically go through their day without giving their actions and reactions a second thought. As they say, many of us "don't stop to smell the roses." Instead we tend to walk right past them en route to our next destination.

The result of this type of lifestyle is that many people do not know what they need in life. They are not sure what they need to do for themselves to fulfill their desires and to ensure they are taking good care of themselves. It stands to reason that they also do not know what they need from their spouses so they can meet their needs as well.

Some of my patients have told me that they consider thinking of their own needs as being selfish. They believe their purpose in life is to attend to the needs of others and to make sure their needs are met. They believe the needs of their spouse, parents, children, and those of their employer are the most important. After all is said and done, they may consider attending to what they need, if they have the time, energy, or understanding of how to do so.

The Needs Notebook Helps to Establish Healthy Boundaries

To establish healthy boundaries, we must be aware of our needs. Then we can state them succinctly in a *Needs Notebook*. By creating a *Needs Notebook*, a couple can begin to establish healthy boundaries in their relationship. We have observed that low self-esteem, fear of losing a love interest, fear of rejection, or being intimidated by a manipulative partner often prevents a person from stating his or her needs and preferences. What occurs too often is that boundaries become skewed, and the power in a given relationship is out of balance. A spouse may exhibit behaviors that undermine the relationship by inadvertently violating unsaid boundaries. A partner may choose to allow his spouse to continue this behavior to avoid his discomfort with confrontation or ultimate fear of rejection. For example, a spouse may know his wife is having an affair. He may choose to remain silent or resist telling her to end the affair for fear that she will leave him. He may believe a cheating wife is better than no wife at all. This spouse's low self-esteem and unsaid boundaries make him feel unable to speak his mind and state his need for a monogamous relationship with his wife.

We have met spouses who were so intimidated by their mates they allowed unhealthy boundaries to continue indefinitely. When one spouse is terribly controlling and demanding, the other spouse may be fearful of making her needs known. This is especially the case if there is continued abuse or threatening behavior in the relationship.

In chapter 6 we discussed the need for a balance of power in a healthy relationship. If one spouse controls the decisions about their joint finances, what car to buy, whether the spouse is allowed to buy a new blouse for a special occasion, the way the household is run, and also expects to be consulted regarding other decisions as well, then the balance of power has been shifted too drastically to one side. The controlling spouse has stepped over the boundaries of respect and consideration for his spouse. Consequently, the controlling spouse probably has needs met, but the needs of the controlled spouse are not met. The spouse that is controlled will in all probability grow to feel resentful and angry. The *Needs Notebook* provides the couple with a detailed guide that specifies what each spouse needs. This helps to prevent an unbalanced relationship in which poor boundaries exist.

Some spouses believe they must not state their needs for fear they will appear too demanding or controlling. They are individuals who tend to yield to others to keep the peace in their relationships. They don't like to disturb their spouses or make too many demands. They may fear rejection, retaliation, or confrontation with their spouse and others. When these passive partners are upset, they may either choose to remain silent, or may become *passive aggressive* by exhibiting behaviors that are indirectly hostile and defiant. An example would be "forgetting" to purchase a birthday gift for a spouse, or gossiping to others about their negative feelings toward their spouse, rather than express these feelings directly to the spouse in question. They may exhibit other potentially harmful or hurtful acts that serve to indirectly express their discontent. The *Needs Notebook* allows the silent partners of this world an appropriate outlet where they can voice their needs and expectations in their relationships with others.

THE CONFLICT RESOLUTION NOTEBOOK

In chapter 4 we discussed the usefulness of the *Conflict Resolution Notebook.* Couples who have effectively mastered our conflict resolution techniques are better able to solve previously unresolved issues, current difficulties, as well as prevent future conflict areas. It may be ambitious to say that mastering these techniques can help a couple reach into the future and prevent problems from occurring. Naturally we do not use a crystal ball to predict what stressors our patients will encounter that will test their resolve as a couple. Instead, we are stating that by using our techniques, couples learn to increase their knowledge and awareness of how to manage triggers that spark arguments and conflicts. This knowledge and awareness together with experience and skill in immediately resolving conflicts before they worsen is an important goal in our marital and relationship therapy. Once our patients have learned these skills, we have noticed that they become more confident and communicative with each other. They have learned how to effectively discuss important concerns without fear of getting into an argument or putting their relationship in jeopardy.

In learning effective conflict resolution skills, our couples can disagree without fighting. Instead, they learn to agree to disagree. Our couples learn how to state their feelings and opinions concisely in a calm, focused, rational manner. They learn how to compromise without feeling defeated, how to listen accurately, and to be more patient with each other. These skills are both important and useful since our couples can take them from the bedroom to the boardroom. We believe many of the skills we teach in relationship therapy with our couples are also effective in interactions with neighbors, co-workers, parents, children, siblings, and friends.

The Conflict Resolution Notebook Helps Resolve Conflicts without Fighting

We recommend that when attempting to resolve a conflict, it is important to focus on one problem area at a time. We advise our couples that if the issue involves buying a car, do not use this opportunity to discuss your discontent that certain chores are not being done on a timely basis. If the problem is whether you can afford to go on a vacation this month, then do not discuss an argument you had last winter about your mother-in-law. We know that many current problems awaken memories of past conflicts. Nevertheless, it is best to not bring old issues into new discussions that deserve immediate attention. We also recommend that our couples avoid phrases such as *you always*, or *you never*, or any other statement that serves to generalize from one issue to another. We ask our couples to not exaggerate the importance of the issue, or what has actually happened that makes the issue something they need to discuss at that time. We tell our couples to stick to the facts and to use *I* statements when describing how they feel about what they have experienced. In addition, we remind our couples to avoid what we have described earlier in our book as *tit for tat* arguments. They are used to prove the spouse has done something worse to them than they have done to their spouse. They are used to prove they are even more hurt than their spouse has ever been in their relationship. We repeat, *it is not a competition, it is a marriage!*

When discussing an important matter, we ask our couples to choose a place where they can privately discuss a conflict without interruption. We suggest they pick a time when they will not encounter a time crunch. We recommend that our couples omit alcohol, drugs, or any substance that can cloud their judgment and their impulse control. We suggest omitting verbal abuse or physically threatening behaviors when attempting to resolve a conflict, or for that matter, at any other time! We also want our couples to respect each other, and be able to discuss a variety of topics without fear of being abused or hurt.

The Conflict Resolution Notebook's Communication Exercise

Before a couple is able to resolve conflicts, they must communicate more effectively with one another. We accomplish this through a communication exercise we created. The exercise is as follows:

- Spouse A discusses a topic unrelated to the relationship (a newspaper article, book, movie, etc.) with Spouse B.

- Spouse A talks about the topic for three or four minutes while Spouse B listens.

- When Spouse A is finished, Spouse B repeats what Spouse A has just said.

- If Spouse B is correct, Spouse A states this.

- If Spouse Be is incorrect, then Spouse A outlines the miscommunications.

- This process lasts until the topic is fully understood. Then Spouses A and B switch roles.

This exercise allows the couple to practice listening to each other. It also provides an excellent opportunity for the couple to give and accept appropriate feedback.

The Conflict Resolution Notebook Exercises

After the communication exercises are practiced and successfully completed, the couple is ready to approach *conflict resolution*. When we first teach a conflict resolution exercise, we ask our couples to define conflicts as cold, medium, or hot. A cold conflict might be that one spouse has not replaced the toothpaste cap after brushing his teeth after breakfast that morning, while a hot topic may be that one spouse feels the other is flirtatious with their neighbor.

Unlike the *Needs Notebook*, the *Conflict Resolution Notebook* is created together by both spouses. The following procedure is employed:

- Spouse A will say to Spouse B, "I would like to discuss an issue with you," and tells Spouse B what the issue is.

- Spouse B has the option of discussing the topic in forty-five or ninety minutes. This allows both partners an opportunity to cool off, and time for each person to review the issue and decide how they want to approach the topic that will be discussed. A time lapse also allows each spouse time to explore their own feelings and put them into perspective. They may do some soul searching and try to ascertain why they feel so strongly about a certain issue. The couple then meets at the designated time in a comfortable setting.

- Spouse A describes the issue in its entirety and Spouse B listens.

- When Spouse A is finished, Spouse B says what he heard.

- Spouse A states that Spouse B's assessment of the issue is either correct or incorrect. If the assessment of the issue is incorrect, then the miscommunication is discussed until the couple agrees on the issue that they need to resolve. Once they agree, the issue is written down in the *Conflict Resolution Notebook.*

- At this point Spouse A describes a way to resolve the conflict and Spouse B listens. When A is finished, Spouse B repeats the proposed resolution.

- Spouse A either asserts that Spouse B is correct in understanding the proposed resolution or corrects the miscommunication.

- Once it is clear that Spouse B understands the proposed resolution then Spouse B has the option to either accept the resolution or not to accept it.

- If Spouse B does not accept the resolution, then each spouse may propose other resolutions, until both spouses accept one resolution. If they are unable to agree on a resolution, then they are encouraged to table the discussion until a later time. Once both spouses accept a resolution, then it is filed under the general topic area of the particular conflict. Both sign and date this page and then file it in their *Conflict Resolution Notebook.*

This procedure occurs with every conflict. Eventually the couple has a *Conflict Resolution Notebook* that contains many solutions to their problems. This prevents the couple from having to discuss and resolve the same conflicts over and over again. Instead, they can simply look through their *Conflict Resolution Notebook* to learn how to successfully resolve a given issue. Of course, new resolutions and problem solving ideas can be added to the *Conflict Resolution Notebook* at any time. Similar to the *Needs Notebook*, the *Conflict Resolution Notebook* never has an end or a final chapter. It is a book the couple will continue to add to throughout their lives together. The couple is advised to keep the *Conflict Resolution Notebook* in a central location so it can be easily found when necessary. We recommend that our couples keep it next to the other resource notebooks we recommend so the contents of their resource library are kept together.

Here is an example of an effective conflict resolution exercise between Bart and Paula:

Paula: I have an issue to discuss about my mother's upcoming visit. Would you like to discuss it in forty-five or ninety minutes? Would you like to meet in the living room or the family room?

Bart: I would like to discuss it in forty-five minutes. It is now 7 p.m., I will see you at 7:45 in the family room.

At 7:45 Bart and Paula reconvene in the family room of their house.

Paula: My mother visits approximately twice a year. I realize she can be very critical of us because you work at home and take care of the children while I work full-time outside of the house. We have a system that is working for us, but my mother makes statements that are especially cutting to you. I understand that you get mad at her, but sometimes you carry it too far and yell at her. Last time she was here you called her a "meddling old hag." Then you told her to "pack her bags and leave." I am worried you will yell at my mother and there will be another uncomfortable scene during her upcoming visit.

Bart: You are worried I will lose my temper at your mother for criticizing our agreed-upon system where I stay home, work, and take care of the children, while you work out side of our house?

Paula: Yes, this is what I stated. This is my concern.

Paula then opens up their *Conflict Resolution Notebook*, and proceeds to write the following:

I do not like my mother's cutting statements about our lifestyle. I will be calling her before she arrives and will tell her to refrain from restating her negative opinions about how we live our lives. Once here, if she makes a negative comment to either of us, I will take her aside and will ask her to respect our lifestyle. You may say the same to her, but I ask you to not raise your voice at her, call her names, or ask her to leave.

Bart: I accept this resolution and add that I will leave the room if she insults me. I am also concerned that I will lose my temper at her. I don't want to cause problems between you and your mother.

Paula: If you are angry at my mother and need to leave the room, I will understand.

Both Paula and Bart signed and dated this agreement in their *Conflict Resolution Notebook*. Next time Paula and Bart need to discuss this issue, they can refer to their *Conflict Resolution Notebook* to recall how they decided to resolve it. If they choose, they can add additional ideas on how to address the same issue. They are to both sign and date any addendums to their *Conflict Resolution Notebook*.

DATE NIGHT LOG

We strongly recommend that our couples have date nights once a week or as often as possible. As discussed in chapter 10, each spouse takes turns planning a date for his mate with his or her tastes and preferences in mind. Then the following week, it will be the other spouse's turn to do the same.

The dates could be expensive or inexpensive such as a pizza night at home, a walk to the market for an ice cream cone, an evening out to attend a musical event, or a romantic evening in bed if they choose to do so. Naturally, there is no pressure to end dates in an intimate encounter. At the end of each date, the spouse who planned the date will document what they did on their date in their *Date Night Log*. Both spouses sign and date each entry.

Sample entry in a Date Night Log:

I wrote Sam a note to meet me at the Oak Crest Spa at 7 p.m. on June 3, 2011. Sam arrived on time and met me in the lobby. We were escorted to a room with two massage beds. We held hands as we were massaged. I felt all my stress melt away. We were then brought to another room where we had facials! Sam was a bit embarrassed because it was his first facial. He giggled as they covered his face with a fruity mask. I couldn't help but laugh as well. I pictured Sam lying there with goop all over his face. I think he was trying to lick it off, but his tongue couldn't reach. Sam commented that the mask tasted good, like pineapple! We then romped in the hot tub and drank champagne. That was a great way to end our evening at the spa. Next we went to our local pizza place, and giggled as we discussed our evening at the spa. I will forever remember Sam with the goop all over his face. We went home, paid the babysitter, and told the kids about our fun evening.

Love, Arlene and Sam, June 3, 2011

The purpose of a couples date is to provide them with quality time that may have been missing in their relationship. It allows each spouse an opportunity to show his mate he knows what she likes to do, and that he is thoughtful enough to plan a special date around that particular activity. The date night serves to return the couple to an exciting time when they were just starting their relationship. Together they can recall the fun times they had before they started feeling the stress of their current lives with increased job responsibilities, saving for college educations, and of having their own parents who are in need of much assistance as they grow older. They can recapture their identity as a couple and enjoy just being husband and wife enjoying each other while they enjoy the lives they created together.

RELATIONSHIP MEMORIES NOTEBOOK

We encourage our couples to create happy memories on a daily basis. These are memories they can reflect on in years to come. When a troubled couple looks back through their *Relationship Memories Notebook*, they can recall a happier time in their lives. These pleasant memories can help them recapture days when they were happy and looking forward to their future together.

Items that can be placed in a *Relationship Memories Notebook* include the following:

- Photographs of fun times together
- Souvenirs such as seashells or other small trinkets
- Ticket stubs from theater or concerts
- Napkins or matches from a favorite restaurant
- A drawing depicting a favorite place once visited together
- Diary entries that describe the activities of a fun date together
- Playbills
- Pressed flowers, leaves, or herbs that were from a favorite vacation spot
- A tissue sprayed with perfume or cologne that was worn on the day the couple fell in love
- Love letters sent to each other during special life moments
- Anything small that is won at a carnival or other memento that is special to the couple

The couple is asked to sign and date each entry and write a small paragraph about what was special about that particular day. It is a good idea to place the entries in date order. You will want the *Relationship Memories Notebook* to be a tribute to the lives you are enjoying together. Be sure to write the names of every one who participated in the fun event. The *Relationship Memories*

Notebook will be a treasured album of your lives together. It will tell a story of who you are as a couple. It will remind you of what you looked like together as a couple in various locations. Whether you are on vacation in Europe or shopping in your hometown, there will be pictures of your time together, smiling, laughing, hugging, or kissing. These are the memories that will bring you and those you love joy forever and for generations to come. Enjoy!

FAMILY MEETING BOOK

We encourage our couples and their children to have family meetings once a week. In each meeting, someone is designated to be the recorder of the meeting minutes. The minutes of the meetings go into the *Family Meeting Book*. In a family meeting, the minutes from that past week are read. The family is asked to discuss their schedule for the upcoming week. This relates to any trips they are taking out of town for business or pleasure; events occurring such as baseball games, concerts, piano lessons, and doctors appointments. It will also include events at home such as scheduled visitors, repairs that will be performed, parties that are forthcoming, and so forth.

All of these events go in the meeting minutes as well as on a family calendar, or if you choose, a dry erase board. The family calendar also contains events that will occur in the future such as graduations, weddings, and family trips or vacations. The family calendar is kept in a central location and is discussed and updated in the weekly family meetings.

In the family meeting, the couple also discusses the chores that must be completed that week. We recommend the couple create a chore list that includes the specific chore, who is assigned to complete it, and the date the chore is due to be completed. If the chores were not completed, a discussion takes place in the family meeting regarding the reasons why they were not done.

The family meeting is also a time for everyone to touch base and discuss what is going on in their relationship. Now is the time to address concerns as well as celebrations of accomplishments made that week such as good grades in school, a job promotion, a completed report, a compliment from a neighbor on how great the garden looks, the purchase of something new and exciting, and so forth. The celebration can include praise for the person who completed an important task, applause, and perhaps a small party with popcorn and jellybeans!

In therapy we may review some aspects of the couple's resource library. We encourage the couple to maintain the notebooks we discussed since they contain useful information for their relationship. We remind them to add current entries to their books so they are always up to date. We believe that the resource library greatly enhances a couple's ability to relate to each other. It increases cooperative communication, awareness of each other's needs, and is often fun to create. The couple has license to make the notebooks as artistic, colorful, and interesting as their imagination allows them to be. The creation of the resource library is truly a partnership in the making.

Chapter Twelve

Planning for the Future

As our couples progress in therapy, they learn various tools and techniques that improve their relationships. We emphasize teaching skills that happy couples have mastered along the way. Happy couples are our mentors. They are our tour guides in the world of successful relationships.

Happy Couples Needing Solutions

Happy couples are adept at recognizing their relationships need improvement. They are quick to come into therapy for the help they need before their minor problems become more complicated. They report they are cognizant of a need for a change in their lives. They may state they do not have the same comfort with each other as they did when they first got together. They may feel the stressors in their lives are interfering with their relationships. They may fear they are drifting apart. This is a danger signal they respond to. It is a cry for help and a need for a change. To address this signal, they summon up the courage to ask for help. These couples truly want to change. Together they accept responsibility for the difficult issues they are facing in their relationship. They come to us to accept the challenge that marital therapy brings. Their desire is to take their relationships to another level, one that is more satisfying and carries the promise of the future success of their marriage.

As we get to know our couples, we continually assess for what went wrong in their relationships. We observe their interactions and ascertain where we must start in order to increase their comfort level with each other. We may begin with helping our couples to review how to communicate with each other by using techniques that are new and exciting to them. We enjoy seeing couples express a new realization of hope that their relationships can improve. They can use a more understanding and civil tone of vocabulary and voice with each other. They can improve their ability to listen effectively, without the need to compete with each other for attention and power.

Our couples tend to be eager to learn more effective ways to address their conflicts. They are tired of fighting. They want to stop shouting at each other. They want to be able to resolve their issues amicably, yet without losing face or giving up their personal dignity. We help them learn and eventually master effective conflict resolution skills that they will record in a *Conflict Resolution Notebook*. As stated in chapter 11, this becomes their personal guide to successfully ending conflicts when they occur.

We realize happy couples have a solid foundation of love, respect, and compatibility. We cannot teach a couple to become compatible if they simply do not fit together for a variety of reasons. Yet our couples that share fundamental values, ethical practices, physical attraction, personal habits, and a strong sense of belonging together can benefit from our martial therapy sessions when overwhelming obstacles threaten their relationships.

Each couple we meet has different goals for their relationship. Our goal for all of our couples is to learn to respect themselves as well as each other. We help them to develop an honest and open relationship without fear of being judged or rejected. We teach our couples to create realistic goals and expectations of one another. We encourage our couples to play fair and have fun both today and in the years to come.

The spouses we see in therapy enjoy growing stronger together as couples. They also benefit from personal growth. In therapy they learn to be more aware of who they are, what they need, what they want, and what they want to become both as individuals and as couples. We encourage each spouse to create a *Needs Notebook* in which they identify what they need their mate to do in a variety of situations. This exercise helps our couples avoid playing mind reader when interacting with each other. It takes the guesswork out of knowing how to please one another. This makes life easier, indeed!

As our couples progress in therapy, they learn constructive ways to share their ideas and to both provide and accept feed back from each other. They learn to be helpful to one another. They become more proficient at keeping their expectations of each other realistic and reasonable. What's more, they avoid becoming defensive and ready to attack when they get fair and constructive input from their spouses.

With continued therapy, our couples become more capable of setting realistic goals for themselves, their marital partners, and for their relationship in general. They may realize that they previously had unrealistic expectations that were placing extraordinary demands on their spouses. They learn to recognize the sources of these expectations and to replace them with attainable dreams.

Our successful couples become more comfortable with physical closeness. They begin to share more sensual and sexual experiences that further enhance their interactions with each other. Together they learn skills and techniques that lead to more satisfaction with each other.

Maintaining Progress

As we see our couples progress in therapy, we ask them to make lists of ways they can maintain the progress they have made thus far. This list is usually comprised of issues related to communication and respect. A sample list includes the following:

* Continue to enter items in our resource library, and review them regularly
* Respect my spouse's need for quiet time after work
* Be fair and respectful when giving feedback
* Don't interrupt my spouse when he is trying to speak to me
* Ask my wife for her opinion before making decisions
* Stop yelling when I get mad
* Offer to help out more with the yard work
* Review our monthly bills with my spouse
* Don't pout when my husband does not want to go out on Saturday night
* Say "I love you" everyday

When our couples are able to resolve their problems, one by one, they are weaned off of therapy. Instead of meeting once a week, they may begin to meet less often. They may go to therapy twice a month, then once a month, to every other month. Eventually the couple may meet once or twice a year for a booster session. Sometimes couples return to therapy when new problems surface or old problems return. We recommend couples initiate or return to therapy if their problems have persisted for at least three months, and if they have not been able to resolve these concerns to their satisfaction.

In chapter 1 we stated, "you cannot fight until you are ready to lose." We have met with many couples who fought the good fight. They faithfully attended marital or relationship therapy. They utilized all of our techniques and fought hard for their relationship. They were eager to rise above the temptation of calling it quits when the relationship got too difficult and they were tired of fighting. At times they knew there was a choice: go their separate ways or keep fighting.

Although some of our couples decided to stop fighting and left the battle. They did not divorce or go their separate ways because they didn't fight hard enough or give therapy a chance. Rather they lacked compatibility, that *je ne sais quoi* that allows couples to survive marital woes. These couples were happier apart than together. They needed to part so they could move forward in their own lives and explore new goals and adventures. They were not less successful than the couples that stayed together. They just chose a different path, one more meaningful for them.

Those who stayed together decided being together was far better than being apart. They could not imagine life without each other. They looked forward to waking up each day with the opportunity to learn more about each other and improve their relationship. They eagerly anticipated our sessions so they could learn more about how to improve their behavior and interactions with their partners. They welcomed the feedback and the homework we gave them because these efforts brought them closer to their goal: being happy and healthy together.

We have taught these couples to celebrate their lives together, to make each day count. To create lasting positive memories to remember and cherish as they plan for the future, together!

Bibliography

Bancroft, Lundy, Patrissi, Joe. *Should I Stay or Should I Go? A Guide to Knowing if Your Relationship Can and Should Be Saved.* New York: The Berkeley Publishing Group, 2011.

Bartlein, Barbara. *Marriage Makeover: Simple Ways to Revitalize Your Relationship without Your Spouse Even Knowing.* Nashville: Turner Publishing Company, 2011.

Bloom, Charlie & Linda. *Secrets of Great Marriage: Real Truth About Real Couples About Lasting Love.* Novato, California: New World Library. 2010.

Godek, J.P. Gregory. *1001 Ways to Be Romantic.* Boston: Casablanca Press, Inc., 1993.

Gottman, M. John. *The Marriage Clinic: A Scientifically Based Marital Therapy.* New York: Norton Professional Books, 1999.

Gottman, M. John, DeClaire, Joan. *The Relationship Cure: The Five Step Guide to Strengthening Your Marriage, Family, and Friendships.* New York: Three Rivers Press, 2001.

Gottman, M. John. *The Seven Principles of Making Marriage Work.* New York: Three Rivers Press, 1999.

Hendrix, Harville. *Getting the Love You Want.* New York: St. Martins Griffin, 2008.

Johnson, Sue. *Hold Me Tight: Seven Conversations for A Lifetime of Love.* New York: Little, Brown & Company, 2008.

Kuriansky, Judy. *The Complete Idiot's Guide to a Healthy Relationship.* New York: Alpha Books, 1998.

Markman, J. Howard; Scott, M. Stanley; Blumberg, L. Susan; Jenkins, H. Natalie; Whiteley, Carol. *12 Hours to a Great Marriage: A Step-By-Step Guide for Making Love Last.* San Francisco: Jossey-Bass, 2004.

Markham, J. Howard; Scott, M. Stanley; Blumberg, L. Susan. *Fighting for Your Marriage.* San Francisco: Jossey-Bass, 2010.

Stoppard, Miriam. *The Magic of Sex: The Book that Really Tells Men about Women and Women about Men.* New York: D.K. Publishing, Inc., 1991.

Weeks, R. Gerald; Odell, Mark, Methven, Susanne. *If I Had Only Known: Avoiding Communication Mistakes in Couples Therapy.* New York: W.W. Norton Company, Inc. 2005.

Index

About the Author

Dr. Barbara Cohl is a licensed psychologist with over thirty years experience in the field of mental health. She has worked in various settings including: in inpatient, outpatient, and nursing homes.

Currently, Dr. Cohl has a full-time private practice in which she provides treatment for populations including children (over eight years of age), adolescents, individuals, couples, and families. Her interest in marital and relationship therapy, and the numerous individuals and couples she successfully treated, has led to the writing of this book.

Dr. Cohl also has a side practice, which involves creating behavioral programs for owners of challenging cats and dogs. This interest has resulted in her authorship of *A Dog in the Family: A Psychologist's Guide to a Happier, Healthier Relationship with Your Pet* and *A Dog In The Mirror: A Psychologist Looks at How Dogs Reflect Our Personal Family Dynamics,* on the subject of the human/animal bond, and how human interactions with their pets can affect their pet's emotions and behavior. Both books were published in 2005 by Howln Moon Press.

CPSIA information can be obtained at www.ICGtesting.com
Printed in the USA
BVOW031614050312

284389BV00004B/2/P